WINNING CASES
at Grievance Arbitration

JEFFREY SACK, Q.C.

Lancaster House

Lancaster House
1881 Yonge Street
Suite 200
Toronto, Ontario
M4S 3C4
© 2016 by Lancaster House
Revised edition 1994

Canadian Cataloguing in Publication Data

Sack, Jeffrey.
WINNING cases at grievance arbitration.

ISBN 0-920450-06-7

1. Grievance arbitration – Canada.
I. Title.

KE3332.S32 1993 344.71'0189143 C93-093257-9
KF3544.S32 1993

Typeset, printed and bound in Canada

To
Leslie, Lawren and Cybèle

Table
of Contents

II. DURING THE HEARING

III. AFTER THE HEARING

Preface

Advocacy, the art of pleading the cause of another, is not a narrow subject. While every advocate develops a personal style, most would agree that effective advocacy requires varied skills and expertise: the ability to marshall the facts, identify the issues, analyze the law, and develop a coherent theory of the case. A knowledge of the rules of evidence and a sense of trial tactics and strategy are important, as are an understanding of human psychology and the capacity to bring judgment to bear in assessing the strengths and weaknesses of your case. Mastery of the art of presenting evidence and argument is essential, although there is no substitute for thorough investigation and careful preparation.

Much of this book focuses on the techniques of examination and cross-examination. The latter has been referred to by Wigmore, the renowned American authority on the law of evidence, as "the great and permanent contribution of the Anglo-American system of law to improved methods of trial procedure". Professor Wigmore has observed:

> "For two centuries past, the policy of the Anglo-American system of evidence has been to regard the necessity of testing by cross-examination as a vital feature of the law. The belief that no safeguard for testing the value of human statements is comparable to that furnished by cross-examination and the conviction that no statement (unless by special exception) should be used as testimony until it has been probed and sublimated by that test, has found increasing strength in length and in experience.
>
> Not even the abuses, the mishandlings, and the puerilities which are so often found associated with cross-examination have availed to nullify its value. It may be that in more than one sense it takes the place in our system which torture occupied in the medieval system of the civilians. Nevertheless, it is beyond any doubt the greatest legal engine ever invented for the discovery of truth."

The role of cross-examination can, however, be exaggerated. While our expectations have been shaped by televised courtroom dramas, the fact is that it is as rare for a witness in real life to admit to lying as it is common in the episodes of TV's Perry Mason. Often, and especially where a witness is telling the unvarnished truth, not a great deal can be gained through cross-examination, no matter how effective the advocate may be; in these circumstances, cross-examination is more an exercise in damage control. At such times, it is important to remember that cross-examination is not the only, or even the primary, means of contradicting an adversary's case. Of equal, and frequently greater, weight is the evidence you call through your own witnesses.

It is true that arbitrators can fashion their own procedures, and are not bound by the rules of evidence developed by courts of law. However, despite repeated calls for informality and expedition, the rules of evidence which obtain in our common law courts are, with varying degrees of flexibility, applied by grievance arbitrators. This is not surprising when one considers that these rules have been refined over centuries as a means of ensuring a fair trial. More to the point, perhaps, it is the courts which, through judicial review proceedings, determine whether arbitrators have afforded the parties a fair hearing.

There is no question that, in grievance arbitration, as in any other trial process, advocacy makes a difference. Although arbitration is not supposed to be a game designed to test which side has the better representation, the fact is that a party represented by a poorly trained or badly prepared advocate is at a distinct disadvantage. In this regard, where facts are contested and the law is in dispute, the truth has the best chance of emerging, and justice of being done, when both sides have effective representation. May this book, which is addressed to advocates presenting cases at grievance arbitration, serve as a useful guide in achieving that end.

Acknowledgments

I wish to express my appreciation to my colleagues at Sack Goldblatt Mitchell who read this book in manuscript form and made valuable suggestions for improvement.

The Grievance Arbitration Process

Is Arbitration Adjudication?

Grievance arbitration involves the adjudication by a neutral third party of issues relating to the interpretation, application or alleged violation of a collective agreement. It is a substitute for the right to strike during the term of the contract. In short, grievance arbitration is a fair, binding and independent mechanism for resolving labour disputes without a work stoppage.

Is It Public or Private?

Grievance arbitration is both a public and a private process. On the one hand, it is private, in the sense that arbitrators are called upon to interpret and apply the provisions of a collective agreement fashioned by private parties. On the other hand, grievance arbitration has a public aspect, in the sense that it is required by statute in almost every jurisdiction in Canada, and the public has an interest in seeing that it functions properly, in order to ensure stable labour relations. As a result of this public aspect, while ordinarily only the parties involved have an interest in actually attending, the arbitration hearing must be open to the public, including the press, unless the arbitrator is persuaded that there are significant overriding reasons to exclude persons other than the parties. Again, because it is important in the public interest that arbitration operate effectively, courts have acknowledged that arbitrators have inherent powers to fashion remedies for the redress of contract violations, even though those powers may not be set out explicitly in a contract or statute.

Is Arbitration a Contest?

Under our so-called adversarial system of justice, arbitrators do not act as investigators. They do not go out on their own and gather the facts. Instead, they rely on the parties, union and management, to present the evidence on which the decision is based. It is for the parties themselves to adduce the facts by calling witnesses whose testimony is then subject to cross-examination. Each party has a right to present its case and answer the case of the other party. In this way, both parties are aware of all the evidence on which the arbitrator bases a decision, and can satisfy themselves that the decision is a fair one.

On the other hand, because it may not fit within the rules of evidence, or it does not suit the interests of either side to bring it out, the arbitrator is sometimes left in the position of adjudicating a dispute without being apprised of the full background of the case, or the labour relations realities that have driven the matter to arbitration.

What Do Arbitrators Do?

Cases which end up at arbitration require the arbitrator to determine disputed issues of fact and of contract interpretation. In determining factual disputes, arbitrators make findings, on the basis of evidence, in light of the rules relating to burden of proof. In the case of contract interpretation, they determine the meaning of provisions in the collective agreement, in accordance with their apparent purpose, the language used by the parties, and the context of the collective agreement as a whole, considered in light of principles established by arbitrators, i.e. arbitral jurisprudence. Then, they apply the collective agreement, as interpreted, to the facts, as found.

In interpreting the collective agreement, arbitrators attach primary importance to the contractual language used by the parties; evidence of negotiating history and past practice will generally be considered only where the language of the agreement is ambiguous. Even where the collective agreement is not ambiguous, however, a party may be "estopped", i.e. precluded, from insisting on the strict terms of the agreement where it has led the other party to believe that it would not do so, and the other party has relied to its detriment on that representation.

Arbitrators may look to related statutes in interpreting the collective agreement. Legislation can also be taken into account if it is incorporated by reference, i.e. specifically referred to, in the contract. However, even where legislation is not explicitly mentioned, if sections of the collective agreement conflict with statute, the legislative provisions will prevail. Four provinces (British Columbia, Ontario, Quebec and Nova Scotia) authorize arbitrators to apply employment-related legislation in the exercise of their arbitral function. This power may, for example, enable arbitrators to apply human rights legislation in order to impose a duty to accommodate disabled workers, whether or not there is a specific provision in the collective agreement to this effect.

What Powers Do Arbitrators Have?

Arbitrators can fashion their own procedural rules, but they must give the parties a fair hearing: a right to present their own case, and to be informed of the case they have to meet. In order to carry out their responsibilities, arbitrators are given explicit powers by statute, such as the power to accept evidence inadmissible in a court of law, subpoena witnesses, administer an oath, inspect premises, and substitute penalties for those imposed by the employer. Many jurisdictions across Canada authorize arbitrators to extend time limits contained in the collective agreement, relating to the grievance or arbitration procedure, so that a grievance that would otherwise be untimely can be entertained.

Ontario has amended its labour legislation to give arbitrators the power to make interim orders, expedite hearings, direct the giving of particulars and production of documents, and prevent abuse of the process. The same legislation now authorizes Ontario arbitrators to mediate a grievance if the parties consent, and to enforce a written settlement of the grievance. British Columbia has given arbitrators express statutory power to determine pre-hearing matters and make pre-hearing orders. As indicated, in four provinces, arbitrators can apply employment-related legislation.

In addition to statutory powers, arbitrators have certain inherent powers, stemming from the exercise of adjudicative authority, that are not spelled out in statute, such as the power to imply reasonable terms in the collective agreement, and to fashion appropriate remedies in the event a violation is established.

Does Arbitration Work?

Does grievance arbitration work? The answer must surely be an affirmative one, for every year thousands of disputes arising under collective agreements in Canada are resolved without a work stoppage. However, it is less clear whether grievance arbitration is working as well as it should. Arbitration was designed to be a speedy, informal and inexpensive alternative to litigation in the courts. Too often, it is slow, cumbersome and costly. Streamlined procedures, such as expedited arbitration, are clearly desirable, and are now in place in several jurisdictions, including British Columbia, Manitoba and Ontario.

I
BEFORE
THE
HEARING

CHAPTER 1

Processing the Grievance

The Grievance Procedure

Arbitration proceedings are initiated by a grievance, i.e. a complaint, ordinarily in writing, alleging violation of the collective agreement. The grievance should state the basis of the complaint, allege that the action complained of is contrary to the agreement, and set out the relief requested in specific terms. When including a statement regarding the remedies sought, bear in mind that, depending upon the circumstances involved, such relief may include any of the following: a declaration of violation of the collective agreement, a cease and desist order, and a direction to comply in the future; revocation of disciplinary action, reinstatement with seniority, backpay and interest; appointment or promotion with compensation for lost wages and interest, etc.

The nature of the complaint should be set out in the grievance. However, there is no need to refer to particular sections of the collective agreement, in the body of the grievance, unless the agreement itself stipulates that this must be done. If you do refer to particular sections of the agreement, you should include a blanket reference to "other applicable sections", so that the presentation at the arbitration hearing is not restricted to those sections specifically mentioned.

A grievance must ordinarily be based on a violation of the collective agreement. Therefore, before filing a grievance, you must determine which provisions of the agreement have been violated, and in which way. In this regard, it is important to understand that, if the grievance should proceed to arbitration, the arbitrator will determine the meaning of the clause in question primarily by considering the plain meaning of the language used, in the light of its purpose, and in the context of other clauses in the collective agreement. At this early stage, it is useful to review a text or commentary on arbitration law, to assess whether the grievance has merit. Remember that evidence of past practice or negotiating history is relevant only where the language of the agreement is ambiguous, a claim is raised that the opposite party should be "estopped" from insisting on the strict terms of the contract because of a prior representation that it would not do so, or an argument is made that the opposite party has not acted fairly or reasonably in administering the collective agreement.

While occasionally the employer may file a grievance, e.g. relating to a contract interpretation or a claim for damages arising out of an illegal strike, most grievances are filed by employees or the union. Depending upon the type of grievance, e.g. whether it affects an individual or the bargaining unit as a whole, the collective agreement may contain different grievance procedures. In most agreements, these procedures are not mutually exclusive, and the union will be entitled to seek redress for employees in the bargaining unit as well as for itself, but some agreements stipulate that a union or policy grievance cannot be brought if an individual grievance could be filed. In order to avoid a technical objection at arbitration, if doubt exists as to whether a complaint involves an individual or a policy matter, both individual and policy grievances should be filed and processed at the same time. Later, the grievances can be combined, on agreement, or one can be proceeded with and the other held in abeyance or withdrawn. In Ontario, if the statutory procedure for expedited arbitration is used, the Minister of Labour may be asked to appoint the same arbitrator to deal with several differences arising under a collective agreement.

The grievance and arbitration procedure is designed to enable employees to obtain justice at the workplace without resorting to self-help in the form of a refusal to work or a work stoppage. In this regard, arbitrators have ordinarily held that an employee who objects to a work-related direction must in any event comply with the direction, and test the issue of whether it violates the collective agreement by filing a grievance and proceeding, if necessary, to arbitration. Failure to follow this procedure may subject an employee to discipline for insubordination. The "work now, grieve later" rule is an attempt to balance the right of employees to fairness against the employer's interest in maintaining uninterrupted production at the workplace. However, the rule is subject to some important exceptions. It does not apply, for example, in circumstances where the arbitration process would not provide effective redress, as in cases where the order is illegal, unhealthy or unsafe, or constitutes an invasion of privacy or personal dignity. In British

Columbia and Ontario, arbitrators have been given power to make pre-hearing orders, and interim relief may be available pending a full hearing in cases where the grievor would otherwise be prejudiced.

Sample Grievances

Illustrations of sample grievances are set out at the end of this chapter. It should be noted that, while there is no standard grievance form, the form of the grievance must comply with any requirements contained in the collective agreement.

Investigating the Grievance

It is essential to the proper processing of a grievance that the facts be fully and thoroughly investigated at the earliest possible opportunity. As time goes by, memories fade, witnesses leave their employment and cannot be located. They become reluctant to be involved. As a result, you should interview all available witnesses as soon as possible, and make notes of their recollection of events. These notes will be of great assistance during discussion of the matter between the parties, and even more so should the grievance proceed to arbitration: see Chapter 4.

Available documents must also be gathered. These may include seniority lists, medical reports, discipline records, letters of intent, written rules and regulations, previous related grievances and settlements, correspondence between the parties, minutes of meetings, and documents evidencing past practice or negotiating history.

It is useful to prepare an investigation report. The more information, the better. Moreover, the better the information is organized, the more useful it will be. A sample grievance investigation report is set out at the end of this chapter.

Grievance Meetings

Collective agreements commonly provide for a grievance to be processed through several stages before it is submitted to arbitration. Meetings are held at each step, although the number of steps is often abbreviated where a discharge is the subject of the grievance. The purpose of this arrangement is to provide an opportunity to the parties themselves to settle their differences without the necessity for third party intervention. It is usually better to solve problems than to pursue legal disputes. Moreover, grievance meetings provide excellent opportunities to define the issues, and to obtain factual particulars of the opposite party's case, and disclosure of relevant documents.

Be sure to take notes at union-management meetings during the grievance procedure, and to write down not only your own position, but that of the other side. This will help you in further investigation, and in preparing the case for hearing, because you will know what case you have to meet. Moreover, these notes, which should be signed and dated, can be used to acquaint others who subsequently deal with the case, including the advocate at arbitration, with the facts involved, and the positions taken by the parties. You can rely on the confidentiality of these notes, for discussions during the grievance procedure are considered to be privileged, and arbitrators will not require them to be disclosed at the arbitration hearing. To do so, it is felt, would chill such discussions and discourage attempts to settle grievances.

Missing Time Limits—And What To Do

Most collective agreements contain time limits, applicable both to the filing of the grievance and the processing of the grievance from one step to the next, including the final step of referral to arbitration. Replies must also usually be filed within stipulated time limits. Sometimes, time limits are mandatory; sometimes they are not. However, whether or not time limits are mandatory, it is desirable that grievances be processed within the time limits set out in the collective agreement. If more time is needed, an extension of time limits should be requested. This should be done before the time limit expires, and the agreement to extend the time should be confirmed in writing.

What should you do if a grievance is filed late, or there is delay in processing the grievance? The clear answer is that you should proceed anyway, since the time limits set out in the collective agreement may be *directory* rather than *mandatory*, i.e. they may be intended only as guidelines, not as a requirement. Even if the time limit is mandatory, the opposite party may proceed without objection; if an objection is not raised prior to the hearing, the arbitrator may well rule that the objection has been waived. Furthermore, the legislation of some provinces explicitly authorizes an arbitrator in appropriate circumstances to extend the time involved in processing a grievance, whether or not the time limits are mandatory. Thus, section 45(8.3) of Ontario's *Labour Relations Act* empowers an arbitrator to extend time limits where there are reasonable grounds for the extension and the opposite party is not substantially prejudiced.

In short, when it comes to filing or processing a grievance, stay within the time limits. But, if you do breach them, don't just abandon the grievance. There are a number of legal grounds upon which you may be able to overcome the defect. Moreover, if a grievor brings a duty of fair representation complaint, and the labour board directs that the grievance proceed to arbitration, regardless of the time limits, you will have done what you can to limit any liability the board may impose for lost wages due to your delay in processing the grievance.

If the opposite party tells you that the grievance is not valid or arbitrable, don't accept this as necessarily true. Seek advice, or let the arbitrator decide. If the opposite party does not file a reply within the time limits, and the agreement does not provide that the grievance automatically succeeds in such circumstances, you can go on to the next step. You don't have to wait. Remember that processing the grievance—even giving notice to arbitrate—doesn't prevent you from discussing the grievance with the opposite party and from withdrawing it if it later turns out to be without merit. However, if you are going to withdraw a grievance, you should stipulate that withdrawal of the grievance is "without prejudice" and does not constitute acquiescence in or agreement to the action complained of. Better still, if you can, obtain the opposite party's agreement to the "without prejudice" disposition.

Union's Duty of Fair Representation

Eight Canadian jurisdictions have enacted legislation requiring unions to fairly represent all employees in the bargaining unit, and a breach gives an aggrieved employee a right to file a complaint with a labour tribunal. This duty requires a union not to act toward a bargaining unit employee in a manner that is arbitrary, discriminatory or in bad faith. (In Manitoba, unions are also responsible if they fail to take reasonable care in representing dismissed employees.)

For practical purposes, what does this mean? It means that labour boards will not intervene to second-guess union representatives who make judgment calls regarding the merits of a grievance, and that they will not concern themselves with honest mistakes or ordinary negligence. But on the other hand, they will intervene, where a complaint is filed, if a union fails to investigate a grievance, or does so in a perfunctory fashion; processes a grievance in a manner that shows a reckless disregard for the interests of the grievor; treats the grievor differently from others; or exhibits personal hostility toward the grievor, a desire for political revenge, lack of fairness or impartiality, intentional deception, flagrant dishonesty or sinister motives.

Unions have considerable leeway in deciding whether or not to take a grievance to arbitration. They may take into account a wide variety of factors, e.g. the likelihood of success of the grievance at arbitration, the effect of the outcome on the rest of the bargaining unit, the union's financial position, etc. However, the nature of the employee's grievance is significant, for the more serious the issue, the more rigorously a labour board will assess the union's decision not to carry a grievance forward. This is especially the case where critical employment interests are involved, such as seniority and job security.

Unless a collective agreement or statute provides otherwise, an employee cannot go to arbitration without the union's approval. It is the union which is a party to the collective agreement and it is the union which has carriage of the grievance and the final say over access to arbitration. Rarely does a collective agreement allow an employee to trigger the arbitration process, because of the impact an adverse ruling could have on other employees and on the union itself. There are also significant cost implications in proceeding to arbitration which a union is entitled to take into account.

Moreover, as a party to the collective agreement, the union is entitled to settle a grievance on behalf of an employee. This power on the part of the union also reflects the fact that the parties to the collective agreement, i.e. the employer and the union, have a continuing relationship which will suffer if the union brings forward unworthy claims, or adheres to unrealistic positions. There is no general requirement that the grievor consent to a settlement, but as a matter of practice the union should advise the grievor of the terms of a proposed settlement, and permit the grievor to give his or her views on it. However, a union can override the employee's position, if it does so for valid reasons, e.g. if it feels that the proposal is as good as could be obtained at arbitration, or the employee is being unreasonable.

In negotiating a collective agreement, unions may agree to settle or trade off outstanding grievances. This is permissible, provided the union can show that it has considered the merits of each individual grievance, weighed the interests of the grievor against the interests of the rest of the bargaining unit, and arrived at its decision in a fair and unbiased manner. On the other hand, where a grievance involves dismissal or disciplinary sanctions, the discretion of a union to settle an apparently valid grievance during negotiations in order to obtain concessions for the bargaining unit as a whole, without the employee's consent, may be substantially restrained.

Labour boards take note of the fact that union representatives often represent employees at arbitration, and that these representatives are generally capable and experienced. As a result, boards have rejected the argument that the duty of fair representation obliges a union to retain a lawyer to represent them at arbitration. Rather, unions can follow their usual practice with respect to representation, although any departure from usual practice in this area should be justified by the union.

Missing a time limit for filing or processing a grievance will not automatically be found to violate the duty of fair representation. Labour boards take account of prevailing standards in the industrial relations community in establishing standards for the duty of fair representation, and it is a fairly common occurrence for such dates to be inadvertently missed. In assessing complaints of this kind, labour boards will consider a number of factors, including the volume of complaints with which the union must contend, the length of the delay, the language of the time limit provision, the consequences of missing the time limit, the level of experience of the union official, and the reasons for missing the time limit. Only in extreme cases, i.e. where a union representative has missed a time limit because he or she failed to give any consideration at all to the grievance, will a union be found to have acted arbitrarily in breach of the duty of fair representation. In short, honest mistakes or simple negligence will not generally be found to breach the duty of fair representation, except in Manitoba, where a standard of reasonable care is required in dealing with dismissal.

If a labour board decides that there has been a violation of the duty of fair representation in processing a grievance, it will attempt to put the grievor in the position he or she would have been in if the union had not breached its duty of fair representation. In some cases, this means that the board will order that the grievance proceed to arbitration, notwithstanding that a breach of the time limits has occurred. In addition, it may direct that the union provide representation or, where a conflict of interest exists, pay for an independent lawyer at arbitration. Where a breach of the duty of fair representation is found, and the parties are directed to proceed to arbitration, labour boards have held that the union is liable for wage loss sustained by the grievor as a result of delays for which the union is responsible, while the employer is liable for the rest.

EMPLOYEE GRIEVANCE

TO: _____*[name and address of employer]*_____

GRIEVOR(S): _____*[name(s)]*_____

UNION: _____*[name of union]*_____

EMPLOYER: _____*[name of employer]*_____

LOCATION: _____*[location, if applicable]*_____

FILED BY: _____*[name of union official]*_____

UNION POSITION: _____

ADDRESS: _____

TELEPHONE AND FAX NUMBER: _____

DATE OF FILING: _____*[date grievance is filed]*_____

GRIEVANCE: I grieve that I have been denied sick leave for absence from work due to an operation and recovery from the operation, contrary to the collective agreement.

REMEDY SOUGHT: Compliance with the collective agreement, including compensation, interest and other appropriate remedies.

DATE: _____

SIGNATURE OF
GRIEVOR(S): _____

EMPLOYEE GRIEVANCE
ALLEGING UNJUST DISCHARGE

DATE: _____

TO: _____ *[name and address of employer]* _____

GRIEVOR(S): _____ *[name(s)]* _____

UNION: _____ *[name of union]* _____

EMPLOYER: _____ *[name of employer]* _____

LOCATION: _____ *[location, if applicable]* _____

FILED BY: _____ *[name of union official]* _____

UNION POSITION: _____

ADDRESS: _____

TELEPHONE AND FAX NUMBER: _____

GRIEVANCE:I grieve that I have been unjustly discharged contrary to the collective agreement.

REMEDY SOUGHT:Reinstatement with full seniority to my position and compensation, interest and other appropriate remedies.

DATE: _____

SIGNATURE OF
GRIEVOR(S): _____

UNION GRIEVANCE

To: _____ *[name and address of employer]* _____

Union: _____ *[name of union]* _____

Location: _____ *[location, if applicable]* _____

Filed by: _____ *[name of union official]* _____

Union Position: _____ *[union position]* _____

Address: _____ *[date grievance is filed]* _____

Telephone and Fax Number: _____

Date of Filing: _____

Grievance: The union grieves that the employer has contracted out the work of the bargaining unit, contrary to the collective agreement.

Remedy Sought: Compliance with the collective agreement, including restoration of bargaining unit work, compensation and other appropriate remedies.

Date: _____

Signature of Union
Representative _____

EMPLOYER GRIEVANCE

To: _____ *[name and address of union]* _____

EMPLOYER: _____ *[name of employer]* _____

LOCATION: _____ *[location, if applicable]* _____

FILED BY: _____ *[name of employer official]* _____

POSITION: _____ *[position held by employer official]* _____

ADDRESS: _____ *[date grievance is filed]* _____

TELEPHONE AND FAX NUMBER: _____

DATE OF FILING: _____

GRIEVANCE: The employer grieves that the union has violated the collective agreement by counselling the employees to engage in an illegal strike.

REMEDY SOUGHT: Compliance with the collective agreement, together with compensation, and other appropriate remedies.

DATE: _____

SIGNATURE OF EMPLOYER
REPRESENTATIVE: _____

GRIEVANCE INVESTIGATION REPORT

1. UNION AND UNION REPRESENTATIVES:
   [Set out names, addresses, telephone and fax numbers.]

2. EMPLOYER AND EMPLOYER REPRESENTATIVES:
   [Set out names, addresses, telephone and fax numbers.]

3. GRIEVOR:
   [Set out name, address, telephone and fax number.]

4. GRIEVANCE AND REMEDIES REQUESTED:
   [Explain the basis of the grievance, and attach a copy. Specify the remedies requested, e.g. removal of disciplinary notation, and reinstatement with back pay and no loss of seniority (in the case of discharge); appointment or promotion with compensation for lost wages (in a case of denial of a posted vacancy). In addition to specific relief, a useful catch-all request is for a declaration that the agreement has been violated, and a direction to comply with it forthwith, and in the future.]

5. REPLIES:
   [Summarize the replies to the grievance, and attach copies.]

6. CONTRACT PROVISIONS:
   [Specify the clauses of the collective agreement which you claim have been breached. Explain how. Attach a copy of the collective agreement, together with any side documents, including letters of intent or supplementary understandings, bearing upon the matter.]

7. DESCRIPTION OF INCIDENT/DISPUTE:
   [Describe the incident or the dispute with details, including names, dates, times and places. State what was said by all those involved. Answer the questions: who? what? when? where? why? If the dispute involves a question of interpretation of the contract, set out the differences between the parties.]

Grievance Investigation Report (continued)

8. GRIEVOR'S CIRCUMSTANCES/RECORD:
[Provide details relating to the grievor, and the grievor's seniority, age, personal circumstances, etc. If discipline or discharge is involved, add details relating to the grievor's work or discipline record, including disciplinary notations, grievor's explanations, grievances and grievance settlements.]

9. SUPPLEMENTARY INFORMATION:
In case of discharge or discipline:
[Detail whether other employees have been treated differently in similar circumstances, whether there has been compliance with disciplinary procedures contained in the collective agreement, whether there are mitigating or aggravating circumstances affecting penalty, etc.]

In case of alleged breach of the employer's rules and regulations:
[Provide information as to whether employees received notice of the employer's rules, whether they have been consistently applied, whether they are reasonable, and whether they have been agreed to by the parties.]

In case of an issue regarding the grievor's health:
[Attach copies of medical reports.]

In case of promotion or demotion:
[Supply information regarding the grievor's qualifications and work performance, and if the contract clause involved provides for a competition with other employees, information as to the qualifications and work performance of other competing candidates.]

In case of a dispute regarding interpretation of the contract, in the event that ambiguity is alleged, or an understanding that its terms were not to be strictly applied:
[Give details and documentation of statements made by the parties or their representatives during negotiations, and of past practice, and indicate whether it has been carried on with the knowledge of the parties or their representatives.]

Grievance Investigation Report (continued)

10. GRIEVOR'S STATEMENT:
[Ask the grievor to write full details of the incident on a separate sheet, including dates, times, places and names of persons involved. Suggest to the grievor that he or she try to quote statements made by others. Make sure that the grievor signs and dates the statement. Ask the grievor for any relevant documents. Ask the grievor if there is anything in particular, whether or not it is covered by the grievance, that is causing him or her concern.]

11. WITNESSES AND WITNESSES' STATEMENTS:
[Name all possible witnesses, pro and con, with telephone numbers and addresses. Attach your own notes of witness interviews. If possible, obtain statements from those witnesses, signed and dated, together with copies of any previous statements made by them.]

12. PREVIOUS GRIEVANCES:
[Give details of previous grievances, related settlements, and awards between the same parties dealing with the same or related issues.]

13. COMMUNICATIONS BETWEEN THE PARTIES:
[What positions have both parties taken? Attach notes of labour/ management meetings, and include dates, names of persons present, statements made, and the outcome.]

14. DOCUMENTS:
[Attach correspondence, notices, and other relevant documents.]

DATE: _____

SIGNATURE OF
UNION/EMPLOYER
REPRESENTATIVE: _____

CHAPTER 2

Proceeding to Arbitration

Giving Notice to Arbitrate

If the parties have exhausted all the steps in the grievance procedure established by the collective agreement, and the grievance has not been resolved, one party may notify the other in writing of its desire to refer the grievance to arbitration. If a board of arbitration is to be appointed, the notice should contain the name of the first party's nominee to the board of arbitration. If a sole arbitrator is provided for, the notice to arbitrate should set out the names of proposed arbitrators. A sample notice of referral is to be found at the end of this chapter.

In deciding whether to give notice to arbitrate, you should assess the merits of the grievance. For this purpose, you should review the facts, identify the issues, consult the texts and other sources of arbitration law, and arrive at a conclusion regarding the merits of the case. While there is no requirement to do so, parties sometimes seek an opinion from a lawyer as to whether or not a grievance has sufficient merit to take to arbitration. Provided the lawyer is given all the relevant facts and documents, this step is considered persuasive evidence in the event of an unfair representation complaint, even if there is an error in the legal opinion. However, if the legal advice is subsequently ignored, the decision to do so must be justified.

Appointing the Nominee

Many collective agreements provide for an arbitration board consisting of two nominees and an independent chairperson. Time limits for appointment of nominees are usually contained in the collective agreement. If the opposite party fails to appoint its nominee, labour legislation typically provides that you can request the Minister of Labour or other designated agency to make the appointment.

No one who has a direct interest in the outcome of the case can be appointed as a nominee, since bias would then taint the board's proceedings. Moreover, the courts have held that, because of the appearance of bias, it is objectionable for either the union or the employer to appoint an employee or staff member as a nominee to a grievance arbitration board. Where employees or staff members are appointed as nominees to a grievance arbitration board, the consent of all parties should be obtained and recorded.

Selecting the Arbitrator

Although some provinces have established permanent boards for the adjudication of public sector grievances,[1] unresolved grievance disputes in the private sector are ordinarily referred to an arbitrator or arbitration board selected by agreement of the parties to hear the particular dispute. Only if the parties are unable to agree is an appointment made by the Minister of Labour, or other designated agency. In some industries, the parties have been able to reach a consensus on a permanent arbitrator or panel of arbitrators, and this arrangement is entrenched in their collective agreement. In Ontario, the Labour Ministry's Office of Arbitration will respond to a request for the appointment of an arbitrator by supplying the parties with a list of selected names from a roster of accredited arbitrators, many of whom have been recruited and trained by the Ministry. British Columbia has recently established a Collective Agreement Arbitration Bureau in the Ministry of Labour to train and appoint arbitrators.

The presence of nominees on grievance arbitration boards results in added delays, and the practice of naming sole arbitrators is becoming increasingly common. Indeed, in Ontario, as a result of recent legislation, if the parties do not expressly provide in their collective agreement for a tripartite, i.e. three-person board of arbitration, a single arbitrator will be appointed by the Minister of Labour in the event the parties fail to reach agreement.

Obviously, selection of the arbitrator is a crucial matter, and it is essential that you obtain advice from those with expertise in this field before making or accepting a proposal. You should make inquiries regarding the ability of the arbitrator, his or her perceived fairness

1 Thus, in Ontario, the grievances of provincial government employees are determined by panels of a permanent tribunal, the Grievance Settlement Board. However, grievance arbitration for police and firefighters is conducted by single arbitrators appointed, in the event of a failure to agree, by the Solicitor General. Hospital and nursing home employees, as well as municipal employees, are governed by the arbitration provisions applicable to the private sector under the *Labour Relations Act*.

and impartiality, the facility with which he or she conducts a hearing, and the time ordinarily taken by the arbitrator to deliver an award. You may wish to consult previous awards by an arbitrator to determine the manner in which he or she has dealt with similar issues in the past.

The availability of the arbitrator to commence and conclude a hearing is also a factor. Since able and experienced arbitrators tend to have their hearing days booked well in advance, your options may be limited in the case of a grievance requiring dispatch. In this event, you should make agreement on the arbitrator conditional upon the arbitrator being available within a specified period of time. Cancellations do occur, however, and you should ask a proposed arbitrator to advise you if earlier hearing dates become available through cancellation. Ultimately, if agreement cannot be reached on a capable and fair-minded arbitrator, you may have no choice but to apply to the Minister of Labour or other designated agency to make the appointment.

Expedited Arbitration

In several jurisdictions, including British Columbia, Manitoba and Ontario, the costs and delays of the conventional system of arbitration have led to the establishment of a procedure for expedited arbitration by single arbitrators appointed by the Ministry of Labour or other designated agency. In Ontario, for example, section 46 of the *Labour Relations Act* provides that, notwithstanding the arbitration provision in a collective agreement, a party may request the Minister of Labour to appoint a single arbitrator to hear a grievance, provided the request is not made beyond the time, if any, stipulated in or permitted under the agreement for referring a grievance to arbitration. The request for appointment may be made after the grievance procedure has been exhausted, or after 30 days (14 days in the case of discharge) have elapsed from the time the grievance was first brought to the attention of the other party, whichever first occurs. The arbitrator must begin hearing the matter within 21 days of the receipt of the request for appointment. The use of expedited arbitration in Ontario has expanded rapidly, because of its speed, economy and efficiency, but the conventional system of arbitration remains attractive, since it allows the parties a measure of control over the choice of arbitrator.

In requesting the Minister of Labour to appoint an arbitrator, the forms currently in use in the Province of Ontario are set out at the end of this chapter.

British Columbia has recently amended its labour relations legislation to establish a new system of expedited arbitration. A grievance may be referred to expedited arbitration after the grievance procedure has been exhausted and within 45 days of completion of the steps of the grievance procedure, provided that the time, if any, stipulated in or permitted under the collective agreement for referring the difference to arbitration has not expired. The arbitration hearing must begin within 28 days after the referral to expedited arbitration, and the decision must be made within 21 days after the conclusion of the hearing.

In Manitoba, a grievance may be referred to the Labour Relations Board by either party where the grievance procedure has been exhausted or 30 days (14 days in the case of a dismissal or suspension for more than 30 days) have elapsed from the day the grievance was first brought to the other party's attention, whichever first occurs, but expedited arbitration is not available where the grievance has been referred to arbitration under the collective agreement or the time, if any, stipulated in or permitted under the collective agreement for referring the grievance to arbitration has expired. In the event of a referral to expedited arbitration, the labour board will appoint an arbitrator to hear the matter within 28 days from the date of referral. The arbitrator must issue a decision within 28 days after the conclusion of the hearing (14 days in the case of dismissal or suspension for more than 30 days).

The appointment of a grievance settlement officer is provided for by statute in the case of expedited arbitration in British Columbia, Manitoba and Ontario: see page 38.

Scheduling the Hearing

Hearings ought to be scheduled as quickly as possible, having regard to the need to prepare the case and the availability of all parties involved. If you wish a hearing to be held with dispatch, you should take the initiative in contacting the arbitrator's office, ascertaining available dates for hearing, and co-ordinating hearing dates with other parties. You should also be in a position to advise the arbitrator of how many days the case requires for hearing, and attempt to obtain consecutive dates. If this is not possible, hearing dates should be fixed as close to one another as possible, so that the proceedings can be concluded within a reasonable time.

Notice of Hearing

If an employee other than the grievor could be affected by the outcome of a hearing, make sure that you deliver a notice to that individual stating that he or she is entitled to participate at the hearing and to be represented by counsel (at his or her own expense). Such a notice will be required, for example, where a junior employee has been promoted, despite the grievor's greater seniority, and he or she may be demoted if the grievance is upheld at arbitration. Similarly, notice should be given to another union where, as in the case of a work jurisdiction grievance, the result of the arbitration could have a significant effect on its members.

The notice should set out the names of the parties, and of the arbitrator, a description of the grievance, and the date, time and place of the hearing. It should plainly state what is involved, and warn the employee that, in the event of his or her absence, the case will proceed, without further notice to him or her. The notice should be served sufficiently in advance of the hearing that the individual affected has time to seek advice, retain counsel and prepare submissions.

Notice of Evidence

While arbitrators have a discretion to accept evidence, whether or not it is admissible in a court of law, the rules governing court proceedings are often resorted to as a guideline. Thus, for example, it is important to know that provincial Evidence Acts require that medical reports be served on the opposite party prior to the hearing, if a party seeks to file them without calling the doctor as a witness,[2] and that notice be given to the opposite party prior to the hearing, if a party intends to file business records.[3] In some jurisdictions, experts' reports must be delivered to the opposite party in advance of the hearing, if a party seeks to call the expert as a witness.[4]

Particulars and Production

Prior to the hearing, you may wish to request the opposite party to provide particulars of material facts, and relevant documents in its possession. See Chapter 5.

---

2 Ontario requires 10 days' notice: *Evidence Act*, R.S.O. 1990, c.E.23, section 52. See Appendix 1.

3 Ontario requires 7 days' notice: *Evidence Act*, R.S.O. 1990, c.E.23, section 35. See Appendix 1.

4 Ontario requires that the expert's report be served at least 10 days prior to the commencement of trial: *Rules of Civil Procedure (Ontario Court of Justice)*, R.R.O. 1990, Reg. 194, section 53.03. See Appendix 2.

Adjournments

Arbitration is designed to be expeditious. Once a date for hearing is scheduled, adjournments are not usually granted, unless there is good reason or the other party consents. If you need an adjournment, ask the opposing party's advocate for consent before approaching the arbitrator. Terms may be requested, such as payment of the arbitrator's cancellation fee. If the opposite party does not consent, try to deal with the matter by arranging a conference call with the arbitrator, in order to avoid the expense and inconvenience of a hearing. If an adjournment is granted by the arbitrator, terms may also be imposed.

On rare occasions, a material witness will not appear at the hearing, and you will not be in a position to proceed with other testimony. Should this occur, you may request an adjournment, but it will not usually be granted, unless you can prove that the subpoena has been properly served on the witness in question. Proper service requires that a copy of the subpoena be left with the witness, together with the required witness fee and conduct money: see page 58. Proof of service can be supplied by calling the individual who served the subpoena, or by providing an affidavit of service, which should be prepared in readiness for the hearing, in the event you anticipate the witness' non-attendance.

Grievance Mediation

In some jurisdictions, the Ministry of Labour will make available settlement officers, on an informal basis, to assist in effecting a settlement prior to the hearing. The practice of appointing settlement officers is standard in Ontario if the parties resort to expedited arbitration under the *Labour Relations Act*. In this manner, approximately two-thirds of grievances are settled. Recent amendments to the Ontario Act expressly provide for the appointment of a settlement officer in all cases, whether expedited or not, where either party requests, unless the other party objects. Ontario also allows the parties to make a joint request for med-arb of grievances. Similar legislative amendments in British Columbia provide for settlement officers and a process of med-arb if requested by the parties. In Manitoba, the Ministry of Labour will appoint a grievance mediator upon the request of the labour board in the event of a referral of a grievance to the labour board for expedited arbitration.

Whether or not a mediator is involved, an attempt should be made to settle a grievance before the date of the arbitration hearing. This is often the best time to attempt settlement because the parties face the pressure of a hearing, including the time required for preparation, the cost of witnesses and counsel, and the risk of defeat. By settling well in advance of the hearing, it may be possible to avoid cancellation fees, which are conventionally charged by arbitrators. Even if these cannot be avoided, a settlement is always cheaper than proceeding to litigation. Moreover, with an agreement the hazards of litigation are avoided, although any settlement will involve an element of compromise. If a grievance is settled, minutes of settlement should be drawn up and signed by both parties. The sooner this is done following resolution of the matter, the better, for compromises tend to unravel with the passage of time.

A final attempt may be made to settle the grievance on the day of the arbitration, before the hearing begins. If necessary, the arbitrator can be asked to delay the start of the hearing to allow the parties to engage in settlement discussions. A recess can also be requested during the hearing for the same purpose. Once a grievance is settled, minutes of settlement should be drawn up and signed by both parties. It is generally accepted that arbitrators have jurisdiction to enforce settlements reached during the grievance procedure, but if a settlement is not reached until the arbitration hearing, it is advisable to request the arbitrator to incorporate the terms of the settlement in the order so that enforcement proceedings can be taken in the event of non-compliance. Ontario has recently amended its labour legislation to give arbitrators the express power to enforce a written settlement of a grievance. Sample minutes of settlement appear at the end of this chapter.

NOTICE OF REFERRAL
TO ARBITRATION

Date:

To:

Dear Sir/Madam:

Re: Grievance of *[identify grievance]*

This is to advise that we are proceeding to arbitration with the above grievance. A copy is enclosed.

[if procedure provides for a board of arbitration]

We hereby name *[insert name, address, telephone and fax number of nominee]* as our nominee to the arbitration board. Please advise us of the name of your nominee, together with address, telephone and fax number.

OR

[If procedure provides for a sole arbitrator]

We hereby propose one of the following as sole arbitrator:
[List names and addresses of proposed arbitrators]

We look forward to your prompt reply.

Yours truly,
[Signature of union / employer representative]

CONVENTIONAL ARBITRATION
REQUEST TO MINISTER
TO APPOINT ARBITRATOR—ONTARIO

Date:

To: Office of Arbitration, Ministry of Labour

Dear Sir/Madam:

Re: *[Name of union and name of employer; identify grievance]*

The above-mentioned grievance has been referred to arbitration. Please find enclosed copies of the collective agreement, the grievance and the notice to arbitrate.

[If procedure provides for a board of arbitration]
The parties' nominees have not been able to agree on a chairperson of an arbitration board. We therefore request that a chairperson be appointed, pursuant to s.45 of the Labour Relations Act, to hear the grievance.

The nominees for the parties are:
[names, addresses, telephone and fax numbers].

OR
[If procedure provides for a sole arbitrator]

The parties have been unable to agree on an arbitrator. We therefore request that an arbitrator be appointed, pursuant to section 45 of the Labour Relations Act, to hear the grievance.

The representatives of the union and the employer who may be contacted regarding this grievance are:
[names, addresses, telephone and fax numbers].

Thank you in advance for your attention to this matter.

Yours truly,
[Signature of union / employer representative or nominee]

EXPEDITED ARBITRATION
REQUEST FOR APPOINTMENT
OF SINGLE ARBITRATOR—ONTARIO

To: Minister of Labour

BETWEEN:

_____
[the Employer]

and

_____
[the Trade Union]

The *[Employer or Trade Union]* requests that the Minister of Labour refer a grievance arising under the collective agreement to a single arbitrator to be appointed by the Minister.

In support of this request, the *[Employer or Trade Union]* states as follows:

1. (a) employer's address, telephone number, and fax number:
   (b) name and title of officer, official or agent of employer having knowledge of the grievance:
   (c) trade union's address, telephone number, and fax number:
   (d) name and title of officer, official or agent of trade union having knowledge of the grievance:
   (e) name of the grievor:
   (f) date grievance filed and nature of grievance:

2. A collective agreement was entered into by the above parties and expires on the_____day of_____, 19____.

3. Two copies of the Collective Agreement are attached.
   Two copies of the grievance and any replies are attached.

4. Name(s) and address(es) of any other person(s) interested in or affected by the subject matter of this grievance:

5. Name, address, telephone number and fax number of Counsel for employer (if applicable):
   Name, address, telephone number and fax number of Counsel for union (if applicable):

6. The [Employer or Trade Union] is prepared to meet with a Grievance Mediator and is available on the following dates:

Request for Expedited Arbitration (continued)

CERTIFICATE OF SERVICE

I certify that a completed copy of this request has been delivered *[personally or sent]* by registered mail to the Employer or Trade Union as follows on the_____day of_____, 19____.

[Name and title of officer or agent to whom it was delivered]
[Name of employer / trade union of above]
[Address at which it was delivered]

Dated at_____, this_____day of_____, 19____.

[Name of party making request]
[Title]
[Signature]

NOTICE

(1) Two completed copies of the request accompanied by completed certificates of service must be filed with:
The Director
Office of Arbitration
400 University Avenue, 16th Floor
Toronto, Ontario M7A 1T7
Telephone: (416)326-1300 Facsimile: (416)326-1329
All further communications concerning the request should also be addressed to the Director, Office of Arbitration.

(2) It is the responsibility of both parties to ensure that any other person who may be interested in or affected by the subject of the request be given reasonable notice of the hearing.

(3) The Minister may appoint a Grievance Mediator to endeavour to effect a settlement prior to the hearing by an Arbitrator.

(4) An Arbitrator appointed under s.46 shall commence to hear the matter referred to him/her within twenty-one days after receipt of the request by the Minister on a date set by the Office of Arbitration.

(5) Section 46(4) of the Act requires that an arbitrator be appointed on the request of either party. Any questions as to the arbitrability or timeliness of a grievance may be referred to the Arbitrator who shall have exclusive jurisdiction to hear and determine the matter.

SAMPLE MINUTES
OF SETTLEMENT

IN THE MATTER OF A GRIEVANCE ARBITRATION
CONCERNING   *[Name of Grievor]*

BETWEEN: *[the Employer]*

_____

AND   *[the Trade Union]*

_____

Whereas the grievor filed a grievance dated *[specify date]* respecting *[specify issue]*;

And whereas the parties have agreed to resolve their differences without an arbitration hearing;

The parties agree, in consideration of the mutual promises contained herein, to settle the above grievance on the following terms:

(1) The grievance is hereby resolved;

(2) The grievor shall be appointed/reinstated to the position of *[specify position]* on *[specify date]* without loss of seniority or other benefits;

(3) The Employer shall pay the grievor the amount of *[specify amount]* on the *[specify date]* in full settlement of any monetary claim arising out of the grievance including interest;

(4) The period of the grievor's absence from work shall be counted for the purpose of determining seniority and entitlement to benefits;

(5) *[Optional clause]* This settlement shall be without prejudice to the positions of the parties, and shall not constitute a precedent in any other matter or proceeding;

(6) The terms of this settlement may be enforced as if they constitute part of the collective agreement between the parties

OR

The terms of this settlement may be enforced by arbitration before *[specify name of arbitrator]*.

For the Union: _____ *[Signature of Union Representative]* _____

For the Employer: _____ *[Signature of Employer's Representative]* _____

For the Grievor: _____ *[Signature of Grievor]* _____

Date:

CHAPTER 3

Preparing
the Case

The Essential Steps

The essential steps, in preparing your case for arbitration, include:
- (1) ascertaining the facts;
- (2) identifying the issues;
- (3) developing a theory of the case;
- (4) researching the law;
- (5) obtaining documents and particulars;
- (6) preparation of witnesses;
- (7) composition of opening statement;
- (8) drafting of final argument in advance.

The preceding stages in case preparation do not necessarily take place in the order set out above; often they proceed at the same time, as additional facts are added to the bank of evidence, and refinements are made in the development of your theory of the case. Methods of obtaining documents and preparation of witnesses will be dealt with in chapters that follow.

Organizing the Arbitration Brief

It is sometimes advisable to compile an arbitration brief for your own use. This may well not be necessary where the case is relatively straightforward; however, in a complicated case, or one that will extend over a period of time, an arbitration brief can prove very useful, and will serve as a guide or key to the organization and presentation of your case. The brief, which can be in the form of a binder with dividers and tabs, prefaced by an index, may contain the following:
- (1) index;
- (2) a list of exhibits which should be drawn up as documents are filed;
- (3) the grievance and reply documents;
- (4) relevant provisions of the collective agreement;

(5) a summary of the facts;

(6) a memorandum of law;

(7) a memorandum regarding evidentiary issues that may arise;

(8) points to be made in your opening statement;

(9) points to be made in your closing argument;

(10) a list of matters that must be established by you in evidence, the names of witnesses through which they are to be established, and a description of the documents which specific witnesses should be asked to introduce;

(11) a list of your own witnesses, with statements made by them, or summaries of what they will say;

(12) a list of witnesses you expect will be called by the opposite party, with statements made by them, together with questions you will raise on cross-examination;

(13) copies of relevant documents, organized chronologically, according to topic, or both;

(14) copies of subpoenas and notices requesting particulars or production;

(15) copies of relevant arbitration awards and judicial decisions;

(16) other relevant documents, such as interim rulings, previous legal opinions, etc.

It may be necessary, in order to ensure that your brief remains of manageable size, to include copies of documents in a separate binder, and copies of awards and decisions in a separate casebook or book of authorities.

While you should organize your documents in a topical or chronological order, it will rarely be possible to enter them at the hearing in the same sequence, since they will likely have to be introduced through a number of witnesses. A separate exhibit list should be kept and should be cross-referenced to the documents in your binder as they are introduced. Since the list of exhibits will expand as the hearing proceeds, you should place it opposite to or next after the index in your binder, so that it is readily accessible. You should make sure that you have sufficient copies of documents that are to be filed as exhibits, for yourself, the arbitrator or arbitration board, and the opposing advocate. If the number of exhibits is large, you may wish to consider providing the arbitrator or arbitration board, during the hearing or before argument begins, with an exhibit book and a list of exhibits. You should also provide the arbitrator or arbitration board, and the opposing advocate, with copies of decisions that you rely upon; a casebook or book of authorities should be filed if the decisions are numerous.

Ascertaining the Facts

Ordinarily, in preparing a case for arbitration, you will be provided with the grievance and the reply, the collective agreement, notes of union-management meetings, and on occasion short statements by witnesses, or a summary of the facts. Your initial review of the facts may be sufficient to develop a theory of your case, but it will have to be followed up by a more intensive process of gathering evidence, once you have identified the issues. Techniques of interviewing witnesses, and methods of obtaining documents, are discussed in Chapters 4 and 5.

Identifying the Issues

After you have ascertained the facts—indeed, as you go about doing so—you should attempt to isolate the legal issues. The issue may be as simple as: "Was there just cause for discharge? Was the penalty appropriate to the offence?" But the dispute may involve a difficult question of contract interpretation, and the issues may be more complex. A quick review of a text on arbitration law will help you to recognize the legal issues that may arise. The more you think about the case, the more issues may come to mind. The more issues you can identify, the better prepared you will be. In this regard, you should not neglect the issues and arguments the other side may raise, for you will need to prepare responses to them.

Developing a Theory of the Case

It is essential to the success of your case that you develop a theory that will account for all the facts, and point to a conclusion supportive of your party's position. The theory of the case is a version or characterization of events which puts the conduct of the party you represent in a favourable light, or which fits the facts into a legal context similar to that in which a favourable result was reached in previous arbitration cases. There are, it is true, no perfect cases, but your theory should be more persuasive than your adversary's.

The theory of your case may be no more than that the assault by the grievor was the unconscious behaviour of an alcoholic, rather than a deliberate act of violence, but you must have a theory. It must be based on a solid factual foundation, and take into account the specific language of the collective agreement. You can then decide what facts you have to establish, and which awards and decisions will be helpful to your case. In effect, the theory will serve as a set of directions, which can be amplified and adjusted as you proceed.

In developing a theory, you must attempt to anticipate the theories which may be advanced by your opponent. For this purpose, put yourself in your opponent's shoes, and try to develop the strongest case that could be made against you. Then, shape your own case with a view to overcoming opposing theories. A failure to approach the case in this way will result in unpleasant surprises, and attacks for which you will not be prepared. Anticipation of the attack will enable you to meet it, and fend it off.

Researching the Law

Research of the law takes place at various stages of the grievance procedure, although it becomes more extensive as the case proceeds. Initially, even before a grievance is filed, the law should be researched to determine whether the grievance has any merit. When a decision is made to proceed to arbitration, further legal research will be required in order to assess the chances of success at arbitration. However, if the case does proceed to arbitration, you will need to conduct a careful and thorough research of arbitration law and judicial authorities. As indicated, the principles you derive from this research will help you to identify the issues, develop a theory of the case, and ascertain the facts you have to establish in order to succeed at the end of the day.

To research the law, you should consult texts, digests, commentaries, and case reports. See page 128. You should photocopy, for your own use, relevant passages from texts (with a copy of the title page attached), as well as relevant arbitration awards and judicial authorities, whether they support your case or not. You should make summaries of the cases, under the headings "Facts", "Issues", "Decision".

Then, you should prepare a memorandum of law, setting out the facts, the collective agreement provisions, the issues, the law as it is contained in texts, commentaries and cases, and your conclusions as to the application of the law to the facts in relation to the issues involved. You should reserve the memorandum for your own use, and decide which passages from the texts, and which cases you intend to submit to the arbitrator or arbitration board.

Preparing Your Opening Statement and Final Argument in Advance

It is useful to prepare, in point form, an outline of your opening statement, your submissions regarding preliminary objections, and your final argument, before the case begins. Be prepared, however, to revise your argument in the event of unexpected developments at the hearing. While it is important to anticipate contrary arguments, in the course of your preparation, do not present arguments at the hearing in anticipation of what your opponent may say. Otherwise, you may suggest ideas to your opponent which he or she may not have thought of.

CHAPTER 4

Preparing Witnesses

The Initial Interview

Although you will likely have some knowledge of the facts of the case, from previous investigations completed by others, your major opportunity to gather evidence and prepare the factual basis of the case is through your own interviews of witnesses. These should be conducted as soon as possible after you assume responsibility for the case. In fact, the sooner you interview witnesses, the better, since memories dim with the passage of time. Moreover, the opposing advocate may also be "hot on the trail" of material witnesses, and a witness sometimes forms an attachment to the cause of the advocate who first gains that witness' ear.

At the initial interview, you can take one of two approaches: either you can put specific questions to the witness, or you can ask the witness to tell you everything he or she knows that may be relevant to the case. If you take the first approach, it is useful to ask questions bearing on the following: who? where? what? when? why? If you take the second approach, after asking the witness to describe his or her background and involvement in the grievance, you can proceed by asking the witness for a chronological account of the events in question—specifying names, dates and places—from the time he or she first became involved. Once the witness has given you his or her version in full, with little interruption from yourself, you can explore areas which have not been adequately addressed. You will likely also want to review relevant documents, in the witness' or your own possession, in order to determine whether the witness is in a position to identify them, explain their significance, and introduce them at the hearing.

When you interview witnesses, you should make notes of what they say, and date your notes. They will be essential in helping you to prepare for the hearing, and in reviewing the witness' evidence with him or her before that witness gives evidence. In some cases, especially where the matter is complex and considerable documentation is involved, you should consider asking the witness to prepare a chronological account in writing, with documentation included, in advance of the date scheduled for the interview. This will give the witness an opportunity to review events carefully and at length without the time constraints and pressure inherent in an interview. Such an approach will minimize the risk that the witness may omit something important during the interview, and will also enable you to conduct the interview more efficiently.

While you should put witnesses at their ease, and thank them for their assistance, the initial interview provides you with the opportunity to size up the witness. You must ask yourself: "It is necessary to call this person as a witness? Is his or her evidence helpful to my case? Will he or she be a credible witness who can withstand cross-examination?"

Prepare, Don't Coach

It is improper to "coach" a witness, i.e. suggest what the witness ought to say, but you are entitled to inform the witness of other evidence, in order to refresh the witness' memory, especially if you are satisfied that the witness' memory is lacking. You can explain to the witness the overall theory of the case, point out inconsistencies in his or her evidence, test the witness' memory and opportunities for observation, ask whether the witness is certain of what he or she says, and point out the consequences for the case of the testimony he or she would give. Indeed, you should put to the witness any statements previously made by him or her in order to clear up any contradictions.

Ask for Statements

Should you collect signed statements from your own witnesses? In most cases, you will have only enough time to take your own notes, but there is no question that signed statements can be very useful to you in preparing your case. They can also be used to good effect in attempting to settle a grievance, and if it is not settled, to refresh a witness' memory prior to giving evidence at the hearing.

Communications between solicitor and client are privileged, and thus protected from disclosure. Although courts have not been prepared to extend the solicitor-client privilege to non-lawyers, it would appear that arbitrators are prepared to recognize an analogous privilege for advocates, or else to apply the common law privilege attaching to confidential communications.[5] Not all witnesses are clients, and the solicitor-client privilege cannot, therefore, be claimed by all witnesses. However, where a document or statement is prepared for the purpose of litigation, a privilege can be asserted to protect it from disclosure to the opposite party.

Draw Out The Whole Story

Witnesses have a tendency to "edit out" matters which they consider to be irrelevant, but in fact may not be irrelevant at all. Occasionally, astonishing as it may seem, a witness will not disclose a vital conversation with another person, under the mistaken understanding that, if no one else was present during the conversation, it will not be possible to prove that it took place. "It's just my word against hers", these witnesses think. They do not realize that credibility as between two conflicting witnesses can often be determined by an arbitrator, on the basis of consistency with probabilities, without the necessity for corroboration by a third person. Moreover, statements made by another may be admissible, notwithstanding the rule against hearsay, where they are made by or in the presence of the opposite party.

You should instruct the witness to tell you everything that was said or done, without leaving out anything that may, even remotely, be material, and you will be the judge of whether it is relevant or irrelevant. It will be too late if, following the hearing, a witness tells you something that he or she left out in the interview, and it will do nothing for your morale if your anguished question "Why didn't you tell me?" is met by the response "You didn't ask me".

Advise a witness to reiterate the actual words used, where possible, in relating things which he or she said or was told. When a witness starts out by saying: "X told me that he was constantly harassed", you should interject: "No. Repeat the precise words which X used in telling you that". In short, instruct the witness to quote statements verbatim, rather than report them indirectly as narrative. Why? Because the precise language used is often critical, and nuances can be lost if statements are paraphrased. On the other

5 See *British Columbia Ministry of Transportation* (1991), 13 L.A.C (4th) 190 (Larson); *Canadian Broadcasting Corp.* (1992), 23 L.A.C (4th) 63 (Thorne); *British Columbia and B.C.G.E.U. (Lowery)* (1992), 28 L.A.C. (4th) 237 (Bird)

hand, a witness should not be encouraged to stretch his or her memory beyond its natural limits. Indeed, a witness with too good a memory may be no more credible than a witness whose memory is poor.

It is also important to probe beneath the surface of what is said. Thus, if a witness tells you that he or she has been mistreated by someone else, ask the question: "What reason did they give you for this action?" But then also ask: "Okay. That was the reason given to you. Now, what was the real reason?" Since people often give a pretext for their actions, it is not uncommon for the real reasons to be entirely different. However, a witness may not tell you more than what was said unless you ask.

Question Witnesses Separately

You should interview witnesses separately, so that their version of events is not coloured by what others say. If you interview witnesses together, you run the risk that this will be brought out in cross-examination at the hearing, and the reliability of the witness' testimony will be undermined. Fabrication of evidence, and even collusion, may be suggested. It is true that witnesses, if interviewed together, can help jog each other's memories, but you are free to refresh a witness' memory yourself by putting a version of events given by one witness to another, and asking for confirmation or contradiction. Moreover, in some cases, witnesses feel more at ease in telling their story when they are not in the presence of others, and are free from the unspoken pressure exerted by peers or those in positions of greater authority. Occasionally, you may be surprised by the answers you receive when you open an interview by saying to the witness: "I want you to be frank, and tell me the whole truth, regardless of whom it helps or hurts."

Interview Opposing Witnesses, Too

Most people do not realize that there is no property in a witness. This means that you are free to question not only those witnesses who may support your case, but also those who may testify against it. You should disclose your interest and take care not to suppress evidence or counsel a witness to stay out of the way. If the witness refuses to talk to you, you can raise the witness' refusal to co-operate in cross-examination in an effort to demonstrate bias. You may wish to advise your own witnesses, in the event they are approached by a representative of the opposite party who is preparing the case for arbitration, that they are free to decline to answer any questions, and can say that they have been advised of their right to take this position. It should be noted, however, that it is inappropriate for counsel to communicate directly with the opposite party if that party is represented by counsel, just as it would be inappropriate for counsel for the opposite party to communicate directly with your client.

It is important to interview not only those witnesses who may support your case, but also those who may not. Why? In the first place, you will want to determine what actually occurred, in order to be able to assess the strength of your own case and how you should present it. Second, it is essential that you know the case you will have to meet, so that you can prepare yourself in advance. Third, by interviewing hostile witnesses, you can at least tie their evidence down, so that, if an attempt is made by such a witness to change or embellish his or her evidence at the hearing, you will be in a position to put the witness' prior inconsistent statement to him or her, and thereby undermine the witness' testimony.

If a hostile witness will not give you a signed statement, you should make your own notes, and ask the witness to confirm that he or she has read them, and that they are accurate. If the witness will not do that, read the statement to him or her, if you can, and add a note that he or she confirmed that it was correct. Interviews of hostile witnesses should be conducted by an assistant, if possible, since you may need to call evidence to confirm that the statement was given, if the hostile witness denies making it. In circumstances where you interview a hostile witness yourself, it is advisable to have another person present, who is not involved in the case, so that he or she can testify, if required, that a prior inconsistent statement was in fact given. It will not be possible for you as an advocate to give evidence yourself, unless you assign the advocate's role to another.

The Final Interview

By this point, you should be in a position to decide which witnesses you intend to call, what facts each witness must establish, and which documents each witness will introduce. You may find it necessary to meet with a witness several times, but in all cases a final pre-hearing interview is essential for the purpose of reviewing the evidence to be given at the hearing. Some time may have elapsed since the initial interview, and you will likely want to review with the witness the evidence which he or she gave you previously and which he or she will reiterate under oath. This is perfectly proper, although you may not suggest to a witness what he or she should say. The same guidelines which apply to the initial interview of the witness apply here as well.

It is important that you review with the witness, in advance of the hearing, not only the questions which you will pose in direct examination, but also the questions that may be asked in cross-examination. In this regard, put yourself in the role of the opposing advocate and cross-examine your own witness so that he or she will know what to expect. The witness will appreciate this assistance, and it will allay the fear of cross-examination. Tell the witness that you intend to conduct a dress rehearsal. Then decide, on the basis of your own observation, whether the witness will make a good impression, and whether it is necessary or desirable to call him or her at all.

Caution Your Witnesses

Treat your witnesses courteously. Inform them of the point at which you intend to call them, how much time they are likely to have to wait before giving evidence, and how long their testimony will be likely to last before they are free to leave. Take the mystery out of the process. Explain to the witness that you cannot ask leading questions, that hearsay is not allowed, that facts should be stated, not opinions or conclusions, and that the witness should avoid using vague terms such as "I suppose" or "I guess". Advise the witness of legal terminology that may arise and identify the arbitrator and the opposing advocate so that the witness can address them by name. You should explain the hearing procedure, describe the layout of the hearing room, and mention the possibility that witnesses will be excluded from the hearing room until they give evidence.

Witnesses should be advised to testify slowly, since arbitrators ordinarily take notes in longhand, and to remain silent, if the opposing advocate raises an objection, until the arbitrator makes a ruling. They should speak up, and give their evidence firmly, but politely, and look directly at the arbitrator while testifying. Arbitration proceedings are informal, but there is no doubt that a witness who conveys a sense of self-respect, by his or her appearance, demeanour or tone of voice, will command the respect of the arbitrator. For further information, see Advice to Witnesses, below.

Preparing the Expert Witness

If you intend to call an expert witness, you should obtain information as to his or her qualifications and specialty, explore the factual basis of his or her opinion, determine whether those facts are assumed or need to be proved by other witnesses, and ascertain the expert's opinion. Read the expert's report carefully and make sure you understand it. If you don't, request that the expert recommend a good text on the subject, and study it. Ask your expert to review with you the reports of other experts, if you receive them prior to the hearing. In this regard, Ontario courts require that experts' reports be served on other parties at least 10 days before the commencement of trial.[6]

Advise your expert witness to give his or her evidence in a neutral fashion, to rise above the conflict, and avoid appearing as an advocate in the cause. You should also caution your expert to expect questions relating to bias, and to answer forthrightly if asked whether he or she is being paid, and how much. In order to protect the expert witness from a suggestion that he or she gave the opinion that was sought, you should be in a position to file your letter to the expert, outlining the circumstances and asking for the expert's own opinion.

Map Out Cross-Examination

In advance of the hearing, you should make a list of the witnesses you expect will be called by the opposing party. Compile any statements that have been obtained from these witnesses, including any previous statements made by them. Make a tentative list of the points you want to raise in cross-examination. See Chapter 10 for a more extended discussion of cross-examination.

Plan the Evidence

Make a list of the witnesses you intend to call, and a checklist noting the points you must prove, the witnesses who will testify to them, and the documents to be introduced and by whom they will be introduced. Decide upon the order in which you will call your witnesses. Try to lead off and end with a strong witness. While you must call those witnesses who are necessary to establish your case, do not call several weak witnesses to establish a point if one strong witness will suffice.

6 *Rules of Civil Procedure (Ontario Court of Justice)*, R.R.O. 1990, Reg. 194, section 53.03. See Appendix 2.

Remember: the more witnesses, the more opportunities for inconsistencies to emerge, if not on direct examination, then on cross-examination by the opposing advocate. On the other hand, failure to call a crucial witness can give rise to an adverse inference, i.e. a conclusion that the witness' testimony, if it were given, would not be favourable to your case. Nothing is more upsetting than to receive an award from the arbitrator alluding, in critical terms, to your failure to call a particular witness, when in fact the witness, if called, could have given evidence favourable to your case.

Subpoenas to Witnesses

To ensure the attendance of witnesses, and if necessary to justify their absence from work, you can arrange for the issuance of subpoenas by the arbitrator. If you want a witness to bring documents to the hearing, you should specify them, in what is called a *subpoena duces tecum*. Arbitrators have the power to summons witnesses under labour relations legislation, but the standard procedure for obtaining a subpoena in Ontario is for the parties themselves to draft the form, have the arbitrator sign it, and then make their own arrangements for service.

If a material witness does not attend, and you want to be able to compel his or her attendance, or obtain an adjournment based on non-attendance, you must be in a position to prove proper service. This can be done by filing an affidavit by the person who served the witness with the subpoena, or by calling the person who served the subpoena as a witness to give direct evidence of proper service. To prove proper service, the affidavit of service should set out that a copy of the subpoena was left with the witness, together with the correct amount of witness fee and conduct money or travel allowance in cash (a cheque or money order is not sufficient), and that service was effected within a reasonable period of time prior to the hearing (and not, in some jurisdictions, on a Sunday). The amount of the witness fee and conduct money is not specified in all jurisdictions. In Ontario, labour legislation gives arbitrators the power to summon and enforce the attendance of witnesses in the same manner as a court of record in civil cases, and the practice is to pay witness fees and conduct money according to the scale prescribed by the rules of the Ontario Court of Justice.

A *subpoena duces tecum* cannot be used as an instrument to harass and annoy an opponent. Nor can it be used to go on a "fishing expedition", i.e. to endeavour, not to obtain evidence to support a case, but to discover whether one has a case at all. However, where pre-hearing production is not available, arbitrators have held that a broader scope is to be allowed, provided that the subpoena does not go too far beyond the test of relevance. The subpoena should state with reasonable particularity the documents which are to be produced, and the documents must appear to be relevant to the case. If great numbers of documents are called for, and it appears that they are not sufficiently relevant, an application may be made to quash the subpoena.

A sample summons, and the tariff for witness fees, in use in Ontario are set out on the following pages.

SUMMONS TO
ATTEND HEARING

IN THE MATTER OF the *Labour Relations Act*, R.S.O. 1990, c.L.2;

AND IN THE MATTER OF an arbitration chaired by
[name of arbitrator] between *[names of union and employer]*

AND IN THE MATTER OF the grievance of *[identify grievor]*.

TO:*[Name of witness]*
   [Address for service]

SUMMONS TO WITNESS

YOU ARE HEREBY SUMMONED to attend a hearing before a sole arbitrator/arbitration board in the above matter, commencing at *[time]* on *[date]*, and continuing on *[specify further fixed dates]*, and at any subsequent hearing, at *[location of arbitration hearing]*, to give evidence concerning matters relating thereto and to bring with you all relevant documents in your possession, and in particular: *[material documents should be specified]*.

DATED at *[municipality]* this_____day of_____, 19____.

                                 [Signature of arbitrator]

WITNESS FEES AND EXPENSES—
THE COURT TARIFF—ONTARIO 1993
(Rules of Civil Procedure, Ontario Court of Justice,
R.R.O. 1990, Reg. 194)

Attendance money actually paid to a witness who is entitled to attendance money, to be calculated as follows:

1. Attendance allowance for each
   day of necessary attendance $50.00

2. Travel allowance, where the hearing or examination is held,

   (a) in a city or town in which the witness resides, $3.00 for each day of necessary attendance;

   (b) within 300 kilometres of where the witness resides, 24 cents a kilometre each way from his or her residence to the airport and from the airport to the place of hearing or examination.

   (c) more than 300 kilometres from where the witness resides, the minimum return air fare plus 24 cents a kilometre each way from his or her residence to the airport and from the airport to the place of hearing or examination.

3. Overnight accommodation and meal allowance,
   where the witness resides elsewhere than the place
   of hearing or examination and is required to
   remain overnight, for each overnight stay $75.00

ADVICE TO WITNESSES IN
ARBITRATION PROCEEDINGS

☐ If you are a witness called upon to give evidence at an arbitration hearing, you can expect to give evidence under oath, although you can request to do so by simple affirmation without swearing an oath. The arbitration hearing will be conducted by a single arbitrator or a three-person board of arbitration. The process is informal, and does not have the trappings of a court of law, but at the same time it is adversarial, and the rules of evidence apply. You will be questioned by the advocate who calls you in direct examination, and then you will be questioned by the advocate of the opposite party in cross-examination. You may be re-examined by the advocate calling you to clarify an issue that emerges in cross-examination.

☐ Before you testify, review the facts in your own mind and with the advocate who calls you as a witness. Read over any previous notes or statements you have made before you give evidence.

☐ When you testify, speak in a simple, matter-of-fact fashion. Remember that arbitrators take notes in longhand. Watch the arbitrator to make sure that he or she has finished writing before you go on to your next point. Don't try to memorize your answers. Speak firmly and use your own words. Look at the arbitrator when you testify. Do not nod your head in answer to a question, since a nod cannot be recorded. When you testify, you must be factual. Do not venture opinions unless you are asked to do so.

☐ Handle yourself with dignity, dress appropriately, respond politely, though firmly, to questions, and avoid flippancy. You should ask your advocate to identify the arbitrator and the opposing advocate so that you can address them by name. If one of the advocates raises an objection or the arbitrator intervenes, you should pause in giving your evidence, until advised that you may proceed.

☐ If documents are shown to you to identify, you should, if asked, describe the nature of the document and indicate whether you have authored it or can identify the signature.

☐ When you are cross-examined by the opposing advocate, you should respond directly to the questions, but be brief. Listen carefully to the questions you are asked and answer only those questions. Do not volunteer information not asked of you. Often, a "yes" or "no" answer is all that is called for. If you cannot answer yes or no, say so and explain. Ordinarily, the arbitrator will not allow the opposing advocate to cut short your answer, but if this should occur, your own advocate may clarify the point in re-examination if you indicate that you want to qualify your answer.

☐ Do not become angry, loud or belligerent. A clear, calm, confident approach is required. Do not speak too fast or feel that you have to answer the questions at the speed at which they are asked. Respond at your own pace. Don't look sideways before answering a question. On the other hand, try not to hesitate excessively before answering and do not repeat the question before responding. However, if you do not understand the question, say so and ask the opposing advocate to repeat it. Avoid mannerisms that will give the impression that you are scared, or are not telling the truth.

☐ Be firm, rather than hesitant, in giving your evidence. If you do not know, or do not remember something, e.g. a date, or the precise time, do not be afraid to say "I don't know" or "I don't remember", or "I can only give an estimate", or "I can only remember the gist of what was said". Do not make up an answer if you are not sure, but if you do remember something clearly, don't use words that indicate a vague memory. Don't, for example, say "I *think* X was wearing a blue suit" or "I *guess* I was there" or "I *believe* it was raining". These words suggest that you are not sure.

☐ Answer questions honestly. A lie regarding a small matter will undermine the credibility of all your testimony. Be fair, factual, concrete. Don't exaggerate or argue. Don't try to make debating points. Do not be sarcastic, or quarrelsome. If the opposing advocate attempts to brow-beat you, you will gain the sympathy of the arbitrator. If you attempt, on the other hand, to answer back in kind, you will lose the arbitrator's sympathy, for the arbitrator will conclude that you can handle yourself, and the opposing advocate will have a free hand to take you on. Remain polite, and resist the temptation to respond to provocative comments. However, while it is important not to appear to be arrogant, you do not have to agree with the opposing advocate in order to seem agreeable. Stifle any instinct to be accommodating in order to appease the opposing advocate. Watch out for the honey-coated approach as well as for the rough, aggressive one.

☐ Do not conclude, merely because the opposing advocate suggests something to you, that there is any basis in fact to back it up. The question may simply be designed to test your credibility. For example, the opposing advocate may say "Are you sure X was wearing a blue suit? Are you sure it wasn't brown?" There may be no factual basis for the suggestion. The opposing advocate may simply be trying to shake your confidence. If you are sure, remain firm. If not, then acknowledge it freely.

☐ Do not ask the opposing advocate where he or she is going because it will make your answers appear contrived. Do not, in short, try to figure out the purpose of the question, or argue with the opposing advocate. For example, don't say: "If what you're driving at is that I don't know the colour of X's suit, then I want you to know that I do." It is dangerous for a witness to fence with the opposing advocate. Furthermore, the purpose of the question may be quite different from what you suppose. Thus, the opposing advocate may imply that the answer to a question, e.g. the weather on the date in question, is important to the case when in fact it is quite immaterial. He or she may say "I put to you that you cannot remember whether or not it was raining". It may not matter one way or the other whether you can or not, but if you lie, even about a small matter, it may discredit your entire testimony, whereas, the answer, honestly given, may not matter one way or the other. If you are asked a question with an unpleasant innuendo, ignore the innuendo and give a forthright answer. Thus, if you are asked "Aren't you a friend of the grievor?", answer truthfully. You can add that the relationship has not affected your testimony, if that is the case. Remember: do not rise to the bait.

☐ Sometimes the opposing advocate may pose a trick question. If you are asked: "Did you discuss this case with anyone before the hearing?", do not be afraid to say that you have discussed it with the advocate who called you as a witness. There is nothing wrong in this. It is indeed expected that a party's advocate will review the testimony of a witness with him or her in advance of the hearing. If you are asked what advice, if any, the advocate gave to you, it is not inappropriate to say that he or she told you to tell the truth, assuming that is in fact the case. Should the opposing advocate ask whether you are being compensated for lost wages, due to your absence from work, answer frankly. No one expects you to sustain a financial loss in order to testify. If you are asked: "Are you here to support the case of the party calling you as a witness?", you may say, assuming it to be so, that: "I am here to tell the truth".

☐ Under Canadian law, you cannot refuse to answer questions on the ground that the answer may be incriminating, although the answers may not be used in evidence against you in a subsequent proceeding. On the other hand, you do not have to disclose matters which are protected by privilege, e.g. settlement discussions.

☐ Questions may be asked that relate to the matters in issue, or that focus on your credibility—your motives, your powers of memory or observation, previous statements that you have made, your discussions with others, the testimony of other witnesses. Don't say: "Do I have to answer that question?". Remember: your own advocate will object if a question is improper, or you are being badgered. It's his or her job to protect you. Let him or her be the one to do it. If your own advocate does object to a question, do not answer it; wait for the arbitrator to rule that the question is proper before giving your answer.

☐ Witnesses may be excluded from the hearing room. If this occurs, you will be cautioned by the arbitrator not to discuss the evidence you have given with other witnesses until the case is concluded. Your own advocate is not permitted to communicate with you or give you advice while you are under cross-examination.

☐ If you are called as an expert witness, remember to be neutral in giving your evidence, and to rise above the conflict. Do not be an advocate in the cause. You will be asked questions by your own advocate to qualify you as an expert and to describe your specialty. When you give your opinion, you should state the facts and assumptions upon which it is based. You may also be asked to review the opinions of other experts. You can expect, in cross-examination, to be asked questions that probe whether you are biased, such as who is paying you, and how much, and whether you knew in advance the opinion that was sought. You may be asked about the qualifications of other experts, following which you may be faced with opinions given by them to the contrary. You should be prepared to distinguish the opinions of other experts, and to support your own.

CHAPTER 5

Obtaining Documents and Particulars

Requesting Particulars of Facts

Each side is entitled to know the case that it is required to meet. If you are uncertain about the nature of the opposite party's case, as disclosed in the grievance or the reply, you should consider requesting the opposite party to provide you with particulars of material facts in advance of the hearing. In providing particulars, a party is required to provide the material facts relating to each issue in dispute, but it is not obliged to set out the evidence upon which it will be relying. Particulars consist of the times, dates, places, and names of persons involved and a description of the acts complained of, but the names of witnesses need not be supplied.

The opposite party may accede to your request for particulars, especially if it wants to avoid a dispute at the hearing and the possibility of an adjournment, but in the event that you meet with a refusal, write to the arbitrator, before the hearing, requesting an order directing that particulars be given. A copy of your request should be forwarded to the opposite party who will likely argue that the issues are clear, and that particulars are not required. The arbitrator's ruling will decide the matter.

Arbitrators are divided as to whether they have inherent authority to order the giving of particulars *prior* to the start of the hearing.[7] In this regard, British Columbia has amended its labour legislation to confirm the power of arbitrators to make pre-hearing orders, and Ontario has amended its labour legislation to authorize arbitrators to require any party to furnish particulars before or during a hearing.

Requesting Production of Documents

If you have reason to believe that the opposite party has relevant documents in its custody, e.g. attendance records, personnel files,

---

7 Compare *Southern Alberta Institute of Technology* (1992), 28 L.A.C. (4th) 122 (Anderson) and *British Columbia and B.C.G.E.U. (Lowery)* (1992), 28 L.A.C. (14th) 237 (Bird).

notes, memoranda or correspondence, etc., you may want to request production of them in advance of the hearing. In the event that the opposite party refuses to produce them for inspection, you should ask the arbitrator to order production prior to the hearing. As in the case of particulars, arbitrators are not unanimous in their view of the arbitrator's power to order production, in the absence of express legislative authority, before the hearing commences. Again, as in the case of particulars, British Columbia has amended its labour legislation to give arbitrators power to make pre-hearing orders, and Ontario has amended its labour legislation to authorize arbitrators to require any party to produce documents or things that may be relevant to the matter and to do so before or during the hearing.

If you cannot obtain documents from the opposite party prior to the hearing, or you have failed to make such a request until it is too late, or the documents are in the possession of a third party, a little-used, but very effective, means of obtaining such documents lies to hand. You can serve upon the person who has custody of the documents a *subpoena duces tecum* requiring him or her to bring them to the hearing. The documents should be described in the subpoena and proper service must be made by leaving a copy of the subpoena with the individual in question, together with the required witness fee and conduct money.

At the hearing, when it is your turn to present your side of the case, you can obtain these documents by calling the individual under subpoena and asking him or her to deliver them to the arbitrator. If the individual under subpoena denies possession of the documents, he or she can be examined as to their existence and whereabouts. You do not need to have the witness sworn, and thereby run the risk that a potentially hostile witness may be questioned by the opposite party to its advantage. Some of the documents may be helpful as an aid to cross-examination. If you decide to enter them as exhibits, you can introduce them properly through your own witnesses.

The use of the *subpoena duces tecum* to obtain documents is discussed by Arbitrator Bendel in *Winchester District Memorial Hospital* (1990), 8 L.A.C. (4th) 342. See Appendix 3.

II
DURING
THE
HEARING

CHAPTER 6

Procedure
at the Hearing

Arbitration Practice

Arbitrators are obliged to act judicially by giving a fair hearing at which both parties have an opportunity to present their case. However, in doing so, they can fashion their own procedures, and are not required to observe the formalities of a court of law. Thus, whether or not a party will be permitted to have evidence tape-recorded or transcribed by a verbatim court reporter is within the discretion of the arbitrator who has inherent authority to control the proceeding. Ordinarily, subject to the terms of the collective agreement, the parties rely upon their own note-taking, without the benefit of recording equipment.

Appearances

At the start of the hearing, each advocate should file a list of appearances, i.e. a list of the names of those who appear on behalf of that party, and a description of the capacity in which they appear, or of the positions which they hold. You should begin by introducing yourself and the members of your team. It is not, however, necessary to identify the witnesses you intend to call until such time as they give evidence. Advise the arbitrator of the address to which the award should be sent.

Preliminary Objections

If there are preliminary objections, they should be raised at the outset of the hearing. However, if a ruling cannot be handed down without research and consideration of the issue, or the preliminary objection cannot be determined without hearing the evidence on the merits of the case, most arbitrators will reserve on the preliminary objection, and proceed to hear the substance of the grievance. In this way, undue delay can be avoided, and the ruling on the preliminary objection can be included in the final award.

Examples of preliminary objections, and how to handle them, are set out at the end of this chapter.

Exclusion of Witnesses

Before the evidence is called, it is advisable to settle the question of who may remain in the hearing room. Where an issue of credibility is involved, it may be desirable for potential witnesses to be excluded, while others are giving evidence, so that their testimony is not coloured by what they hear. The standard procedure is for arbitrators to exclude witnesses upon the request of either party. Since the exclusion order will apply to witnesses for both sides, you should weigh the advantages and disadvantages before making a request for the exclusion of witnesses. Of course, if the opposite party requests the exclusion of witnesses, you have no choice.

Where an order excluding witnesses is made, who may remain in the hearing room? Each party is ordinarily permitted to retain an individual as an advisor to give instructions to the advocate, even though that person may subsequently be called as a witness. Apart from the advisor, the grievor, although not strictly speaking a party, is almost always permitted to remain, as the person primarily affected by the proceeding. However, where there are two grievors, and credibility is an issue, the arbitrator may exercise his or her discretion to exclude one grievor while the other testifiies: *Toronto Star* (1992), 28 L.A.C. (4th) 444 (Springate).

Other individuals representing the parties may attend as observers, provided they do not testify. In most cases, only the parties or their representatives have an interest in attending a grievance arbitration hearing, but occasionally individuals other than the parties wish to attend; where arbitration is required by statute, the courts have held that the hearing should be open, unless the party requesting a closed hearing can satisfy the arbitrator, who has a discretion, that the proceedings should be conducted *in camera*.

Who Proceeds First?

The order of proceeding is determined by the burden of proof, i.e. the risk of loss in the event of failure to persuade the arbitrator. Generally speaking, the party filing the grievance bears the burden of proof and proceeds with its case first. However, in discharge and discipline cases, the employer bears the ultimate burden of proof as to the existence of just cause. Moreover, if there is no dispute that a collective agreement exists and that discharge or discipline has taken place, the employer is called upon first to present evidence, since it is the employer who has knowledge of the grounds for discharge or discipline, and the grievor is entitled to know the case he or she has to meet. For the same reason, where the grievance challenges the employer's exercise of a discretion, the burden of proceeding first in calling evidence, i.e. the evidentiary burden, may fall upon the employer, even though the union may bear the ultimate burden of proof.

It is certainly desirable to hear in detail the case you have to meet before calling your own witnesses. Nonetheless, there are advantages in going first, even if the opposite party does bear the burden of proof. You have the opportunity to make the initial impression, and if your evidence is persuasive, it may be difficult for the other side to displace that impression. Second, by proceeding first, you have the last word, since you are entitled to call evidence and present argument in reply. The value of this right cannot be underestimated.

You Can't Split Your Case

Bear in mind, however, that if you proceed first, you cannot split your case, and thereby prevent the opposite party from making a proper defence. While you can call reply evidence to contradict or qualify new facts or issues raised in defence, you cannot adduce confirmatory evidence to bolster a case you have failed to make in the first instance, or shore up a case that has been shaken by your adversary. Thus, if you do proceed first, you should make sure to prove the essential elements of your case, and to call whatever corroborative evidence you intend to present.

Splitting the case is to be distinguished from separating the issue of liability ("did the grievor do it?") in a discipline or discharge case from issue of penalty ("does the grievor's conduct warrant discharge?"). In most cases, the evidence regarding these issues is adduced at the same time. However, where the grievor has a lengthy adverse record, the union's advocate may request that the arbitrator determine the issue of liability before dealing with the issue of penalty. In this way, the grievor's record will not prejudice the arbitrator's determination of whether a "culminating incident" has occurred.

The Order of Calling Witnesses

The parties are entitled to make opening statements. Following these statements, the party leading off calls its witnesses, and examines them in chief, one by one. Each witness is cross-examined by the opposing advocate, and can be re-examined by the advocate who called the witness. After the party leading off has presented its witnesses, the opposite party has the opportunity to call witnesses of its own. These witnesses are also subject to cross-examination, and may be re-examined by the advocate who called them. Once again, the advocate who led off has a right to call witnesses, although only in reply to new points raised by the opposite party. Again, these witnesses are subject to cross-examination, and can in turn be re-examined.

Where an order is made excluding witnesses, the grievor should be called first, so that it cannot later be argued by the opposing advocate that the grievor's evidence has been coloured by the testimony of other witnesses. If witnesses are not excluded, it is up to each advocate to determine the order in which to call them. Bear in mind, however, that if witnesses are called after they hear the evidence of others, the weight of their testimony may be undermined.

Calling the Grievor

Where the employer presents its evidence first, as in the case of a discharge grievance, can the employer call the grievor as its witness? Several arbitrators have held that it would be a violation of the rules of natural justice and basic arbitration principles to permit the employer to call the grievor before he or she knows the case that must be met. These arbitrators will not permit the grievor to be called as a witness by the employer provided that the union undertakes to call the grievor as its own witness. In jurisdictions where arbitrators do permit the employer to call the grievor as its first witness, the cross-examination of the grievor by his or her advocate is ordinarily postponed until the grievor has had an opportunity to hear the rest of the evidence.

Is it always necessary or advisable that a union call the grievor in a discipline or discharge case? This will depend upon the strength of the employer's case, and the risk resulting from the grievor giving evidence. If the grievor has admitted the alleged misconduct to the union's advocate, or the grievor's testimony is likely to be destroyed on cross-examination, the union's advocate may choose not to call the grievor and to put the employer to the strict proof of its case. This is a tough decision to make, and it is not uncommon in such circumstances for the union's advocate, in recommending that the grievor not testify, to obtain written instructions from the grievor.

Moving for Non-Suit

If the opposite party proceeds first, you should ask yourself, after your adversary's case is closed, whether you are in a position to request a "non-suit", i.e., argue that the opposite party has not proved the essential elements of its case or, as lawyers say, has not made out a *prima facie* case. You can argue that it is unfair to expect your party to respond to allegations that are not supported by the evidence. Moreover, if your evidence would take considerable time to adduce, you can point out that a non-suit will avoid a lengthy, protracted hearing with its attendant expense.

However, if you move for a non-suit, most arbitrators will require you to make an election as to whether to call evidence or not, and if you lose the motion, you will not be allowed to change your mind. Putting the party moving for a non-suit to an election has several purposes: it eliminates the delay that would result from the arbitrator adjourning to consider the motion, and then reconvening the hearing if the motion is not granted; it prevents the unfairness that would be caused by the arbitrator making an interim assessment of the case; it discourages the parties from short-circuiting the adjudication of the grievance. It is particularly important, in an ongoing relationship, such as that between parties to a collective agreement, that grievances be decided on their merits, rather than by a technical knock-out.

In any event, the opportunity to non-suit is rare, and the risk of electing not to call evidence is substantial, so that the decision to move for a non-suit should be taken only in the clearest of cases.

Presenting Argument

After the evidence has been adduced, both parties present their final argument. The party which led off presents its argument first, the opposite party presents its argument in rebuttal, and the party which led off replies to new points raised in rebuttal. The matter is then left to the arbitrator or arbitration board to decide. Normally, a decision is reserved, so that the arbitrator or arbitration board can consider the evidence and arguments at length. An award is then issued in writing to the parties, upholding or dismissing the grievance.

Closing Your Case

Once you close your case, whether it be in defence or, if you go first, in reply, you will not be permitted to present further evidence unless the arbitrator gives permission. Such permission is granted sparingly since the desirability of hearing all relevant evidence must be balanced against the importance of finality and the unfairness to the opposite party. Most arbitrators require that a party seeking to re-open the case establish that the evidence could not have been obtained with reasonable diligence prior to the hearing, and that it is of sufficient importance to affect the outcome of the case. Second thoughts based on hindsight will not suffice. While some arbitrators are more flexible, there is no question that the criteria for re-opening the case become more stringent as time elapses. Once an award is issued, the arbitrator may have no jurisdiction to re-open the case, even if he or she wishes to permit it.

PRELIMINARY OBJECTIONS
AND HOW TO HANDLE THEM

OBJECTION	RESPONSE
☐ The time limits have been breached.	☐ No, they have not. *or* The time limits are not mandatory, but directory, i.e. a guideline only. *or* Even if the time limits have been breached, the breach has been waived since the objection has not been raised before the hearing. *or* *(In certain provinces)* the labour legislation allows the arbitrator to extend the time limits if there is no prejudice to the opposite party. *or* Where the grievance relates to a continuing or recurring course of conduct, time runs from the last recurrence of the violation.
☐ The grievance involves an individual matter and should not have been filed as a union or policy grievance.	☐ The union can file a policy grievance on behalf of individual employees, unless the agreement says that a policy grievance cannot be brought where an individual grievance could have been filed.
☐ The grievance has been withdrawn, abandoned or settled.	☐ The withdrawal, etc. was intended to apply only to the specific instance and was not intended to be of general effect or to govern in the future.
☐ The provision breached is not in the collective agreement, but in a document, such as a letter of intent, that is not part of the collective agreement. Thus, the arbitrator has no jurisdiction to rule on the matter.	☐ The document is part of the collective agreement or is incorporated by a reference in the document or the agreement. *or* The agreement is ambiguous so that the document can be used to interpret it. *or* The letter of intent constitutes a representation giving rise to an estoppel.

4. There is no provision in the collective agreement covering the matter in issue.	4. The collective agreement does contain a provision that covers the matter in issue. *or* The provision in the collective agreement is ambiguous so that past practice can be used to interpret it. *or* The grievance is founded on an argument of estoppel, based on a representation or past practice, that would preclude the opposite party from insisting on the strict terms of the collective agreement. *or* The grievance involves a question of fairness or reasonableness on the part of the employer in administering the provisions of the collective agreement.
5. The nominee is biased because he or she is employed by a party.	5. The parties have consented in writing to the constitution of the board
6. The collective agreement is not a valid one, and only a court can decide the matter.	6. An arbitrator has jurisdiction to decide this question as it is a question of arbitrability.
8. The grievance does not specify the action complained of, or the remedy requested.	8. A grievance should be liberally construed so as to resolve the real matters in dispute.
9. The arbitration hearing should be conducted in private since it is a proceeding between the parties.	9. Since labour legislation requires arbitration, the public has an interest in the process and it should not be conducted in private unless there are compelling reasons for doing so.
10. The arbitrator should adjourn the hearing until the preliminary objection is decided.	10. The prevailing practice is for the arbitrator to reserve on a preliminary objection and proceed to deal with the merits so that delay and expense are not incurred.

CHAPTER 7

Opening Statements

The Essential Elements

An opening statement is a brief outline of what your case is all about. It involves giving a thumbnail sketch of the facts, issues, and conclusions you wish to advance. Do not pass up the opportunity to make an opening statement. This is your chance to set the stage, to frame the issues from your point of view, to present your theory of the case. You can do a great deal at this point to create an atmosphere that will permeate the entire hearing.

If you proceed first, you should begin by filing the basic documents—the grievance, the collective agreement, any replies—while describing the nature of the grievance, and the issue or issues involved in the case. Without an effective definition of the issues, the arbitrator can have very little idea of what to pay attention to, and what to ignore. At the same time, you should indicate the position you take respecting the issues, and refer to the relevant clauses in the collective agreement. In this way, the arbitrator will be able to assess the relevance of the evidence as and when it is subsequently introduced.

At this point in time, your outline of the facts should be very brief, although it is appropriate to stipulate facts that are agreed to or are not in dispute, such as the names and seniority ranking of employees. Occasionally, you will be able to reach agreement with the opposing advocate regarding the facts, and an agreed statement of facts can be filed. You may also be able to agree on the admissibility of certain documents, which can then be filed as exhibits at the outset of the hearing. Be sure to have sufficient copies available for the arbitrator or arbitration board of all documents that may be filed as exhibits. After you conclude your opening statement, the advocate for the opposite party also has an opportunity to make an opening statement. In reply, you may respond to new points raised by your adversary.

Thus, for example, in a discharge case, the advocate for the employer may assert that the grievor was discharged for insubordination by refusing to obey the order of a supervisor. The advocate for the union may respond by stating that the discharge was without just cause because the order was not clearly communicated. In reply, the advocate for the employer may assert that the grievor fully understood the order, and deliberately challenged the authority of the supervisor in the presence of other employees.

Don't Telegraph the Evidence

In delivering your opening statement, it is advisable to present a general outline of your case, but it is not necessary to assist your adversary by disclosing in advance the precise nature of the evidence. Furthermore, if the evidence does not turn out precisely as you have predicted, the opposing advocate will be sure to point out that you have not proved your case. In short, while it is important, in making an opening statement, to present your version of the case, you should be careful in stating what it is that you intend to prove.

Be Flexible

It is not advisable to write out your opening statement verbatim in advance of the hearing. Set out only the essential points you wish to cover. This will enable you to think on your feet and to direct your attention to the arbitrator rather than to your notes. Although you can prepare an arbitration brief for your own use, it is not necessary to file a written brief with the arbitrator. Such a brief may commit you to a position that you may not wish to adopt, once the evidence has been adduced, and it may set out the facts differently from the way they come out at the hearing. This could cause you embarrassment and, occasionally, serious prejudice. It is important to be flexible so that you can accommodate your approach to the direction in which the hearing develops.

Don't Anticipate

Do not attempt to anticipate the case your counterpart may present by responding in advance; you may simply succeed in suggesting ideas which may not have occurred to your adversary or which your adversary may not have intended to argue. Only if you are certain that the opposing advocate will raise a particular argument should you consider a pre-emptive response.

Retain Control

In making an opening statement, it is not necessary to raise your voice. You should be calm, but firm. Make eye contact with the arbitrator, not the opposing advocate. Your opponent may try to shake your confidence at the outset, particularly if he or she senses you are a novice, through bluster, interruptions, and disparaging comments. By all means, object to the interruptions, but do not respond in kind. If you stand your ground, you will gain the respect of the arbitrator while retaining control of your case. Under no circumstances should you allow the opposing advocate to interrupt your opening statement by offering to take over the role of explaining what the case is all about. The explanation will not be a neutral one.

Specify the Remedy

You should conclude your opening statement, if you represent the grievor, by specifying the remedy that you will ultimately be requesting, e.g. in a discharge case, reinstatement with compensation for wages and other benefits lost. In this respect, you may wish to ask the arbitrator to remain *seized* of the case, i.e. reserve jurisdiction, in the event the grievance is upheld, so that the parties can attempt to reach an agreement on the amount of compensation. If there is no agreement, the union will have to call the grievor to testify regarding loss of income, and it will have to prepare the grievor for questions as to whether attempts have been made to lessen or "mitigate" any salary loss by seeking employment elsewhere. In this regard, the grievor should list, in advance of the hearing, the employers from whom he or she has sought employment, the dates of inquiries, and the responses received. The grievor should also provide a summary detailing the period of unemployment, the amount of income lost, including overtime, less remuneration earned elsewhere, and the total of unemployment insurance and other benefits received during any period in which the grievor has been out of work.

CHAPTER 8

The Rules
of Evidence

The Burden of Proof

It is usually the party bringing the grievance who bears the burden of proof. However, this is not always the case. Thus, in a discharge case, the employer bears the burden of proof, since it must establish the existence of just cause. What does it mean to bear the burden of proof? It means simply that the party who bears the burden of proof must prove a particular issue to the arbitrator's satisfaction. If the arbitrator is not persuaded or cannot decide whose version of the facts is true, the party who bears the burden of proof will fail to satisfy the onus upon it. However, the burden of proof does not apply to the determination of questions of law, including the interpretation of collective agreements. Here, regardless of the state of uncertainty that may be created by the parties' arguments, the arbitrator must make a determination, as best as he or she can, as to which interpretation is correct.

The Standard of Proof

In an arbitration case, as in any other civil, i.e. non-criminal, proceeding, the party bearing the burden of proof on an issue must establish, on a balance of probabilities, that its version of the facts is more likely to be true. In the ordinary case, it is sufficient, when the evidence is weighed, to tip the scales, however slightly, in favour of the version alleged. However, where serious misconduct is involved, such as criminal or quasi-criminal behaviour, arbitrators have held that a higher degree of probability is required, given the potential consequences; in such circumstances, the evidence must clearly and cogently establish the facts alleged.

The Arbitrator's Power to Admit Evidence

Arbitrators are generally authorized by labour relations legislation to accept such evidence as they consider proper, whether or not it is admissible in a court of law. Thus, section 45(8.1)(10) of Ontario's *Labour Relations Act* provides that an arbitrator or arbitration board has power "to admit and act upon such oral or written evidence as he, she or it considers proper, whether admissible in a court of law or not".

The Ontario Divisional Court has held that, as a result of the predecessor section 44(8)(c), an arbitration board is not bound by a court's ruling on admissibility in proceedings in which the same evidence has been tendered for admission. Implicit in the section, according to the Court, is a "recognition that arbitration proceedings ought to be conducted less formally than legal proceedings, unencumbered by strict adherence to rules of evidence which may reflect underlying policy considerations wholly inapplicable in the arbitration context".[8] In *Bradco*, the Supreme Court of Canada has held that a similar provision in Newfoundland's *Labour Relations Act* enables arbitrators to relax the rules of evidence; thus the courts are not likely to review the admission of extrinsic evidence relating to past practice or negotiating history, unless the arbitrator's ruling is patently unreasonable, since "the use of extrinsic evidence to interpret a collective agreement is very much in the core area of an arbitrator's function." [8a] See appendices 4, 8.

Nonetheless, arbitrators are not relieved of the duty to act only on evidence which has cogency in law, and it has been held that they cannot rely on extrinsic evidence in the absence of an ambiguity in the collective agreement,[8b] nor can they base a finding of misconduct solely on hearsay evidence,[8c] or take into account information that is not part of the evidence, unless it is a matter of common sense or general knowledge.

Relevance and Exclusionary Rules

The dominant consideration governing the admissibility of evidence is relevance. But not all relevant evidence is admissible. There are exclusionary rules which prevent certain relevant evidence from being admitted. These exclusionary rules fall into several categories: those that exist to promote the search for truth, such as the rule against hearsay; those that exist to promote efficiency, such as the collateral facts rule; and those that exist to promote broader social

8 *Re Greater Niagara Transit Commission and Amalgamated Transit Union, Local 1582* (1987), 43 D.L.R. (4th) 71 (Ont.Div.Ct.); see also *Re City of Toronto and Canadian Union of Public Employees, Local 79* (1982), 133 D.L.R. (3d) 94 (Ont.C.A.), *per* Blair J.A. at 106.

8a *United Brotherhood of Carpenters v. Bradco Construction Ltd.* (1993), 102 D.L.R. (4th) 402 (S.C.C.)

8b *R. v. Barber, ex p. Warehousemen and Miscellaneous Drivers' Union, Local 419.* (1968), 68 D.L.R. (2nd) 682 (Ont. C.A.)

8c *Re Bond and The Queen in the right of New Brunswick* (1992), 95 D.L.R. (4th) 733 (N.B.C.A.)

policies, such as the privilege protecting statements made during the grievance procedure.

The Rule Against Hearsay

While hearsay evidence may be relevant, arbitrators are generally reluctant to admit it, or to ascribe much weight to it if they do admit it, because it cannot be tested through cross-examination. However, the nature of hearsay evidence is commonly misunderstood. According to the rule against hearsay, statements by persons who do not testify are inadmissible *if they are tendered as proof of their truth*. Thus, if A states that he saw B strike C, A is testifying under oath and is subject to cross-examination by C's advocate. A's opportunity to observe the event, his ability to perceive and recall the incident, and his credibility can be challenged by cross-examination, and his testimony is therefore not hearsay. If, on the other hand, A testifies that X told him that B struck C, then A can be cross-examined only on his memory and understanding of what X told him. There is no guarantee of the veracity of X and the trustworthiness of X's statement. X is not under oath and not subject to cross-examination and, therefore, his perception, memory and credibility cannot be tested. Thus, this evidence is usually considered unreliable, and is treated as inadmissible hearsay.

It must be reiterated, however, that the rule against hearsay is applicable only where reported statements are tendered *as evidence of the truth* of the facts contained therein. If such evidence is not presented for this purpose, but for some other relevant purpose—if it is, for example, tendered to show that a party received notice, or to show the state of mind of a person—then the statement is admissible as proof, not of its truth, but that the statement was made. Thus, a report of the statement by the grievor "I am in charge" may be admissible to show the employee's insubordination, although not to prove who was in fact in charge.

Exceptions to the rule against hearsay have been made in the case of hearsay statements that are considered, by their nature, to be reliable. They include admissions, declarations against interest, statements indicating mental or physical state, business records and medical reports, testimony from previous proceedings, and statements contemporaneous with the incidents in question (*res gestae*). The consideration of whether evidence fits into one of these categories, however, may well yield to a more principled approach, for the Supreme Court of Canada has recently liberalized the law of evidence by allowing trial judges a discretion to admit hearsay, even in criminal cases, where the evidence is reliable and it is necessary to receive the evidence in that form.[9] The impact of the Supreme Court's decision has yet to be felt in arbitration law, but the direction is clear.

Business Records

Despite their hearsay nature, business records, such as accident reports or disciplinary notations, are admissible at an arbitration hearing. Like statutory provisions in a number of other jurisdictions in Canada, Ontario's *Evidence Act*[10] allows the admission of business records, if proper notice is given (in Ontario, 7 days), provided the record was made in the usual and ordinary course of business, and it was in the usual and ordinary course of such business to make the writing or record at the time of the act, transaction, occurrence or event or within a reasonable time thereafter.

While arbitrators have a broad discretion under labour relations legislation to accept evidence whether or not it is admissible in a court of law, and there may be no need to comply with statutory notice requirements or other procedures, as a matter of fairness it is appropriate to give the opposite party notice and an opportunity to inspect the records.

At the hearing, the usual practice is to call an individual who has personal knowledge of the operations of the party producing the business records and who is familiar with the circumstances surrounding their preparation. That individual will be able to authenticate the business record so that it can be admitted as evidence. The opposing party is free to challenge the accuracy of the record and can, for this purpose, call the person who made it, and in all probability, cross-examine him or her upon it.

Medical Reports

A medical report is admissible, in the absence of the doctor who wrote it, despite its hearsay nature. This is the effect of Ontario's *Evidence Act*,[11] and similar legislation in other jurisdictions, provided that the required notice is given to the opposite party (in Ontario, 10 days), together with a copy of the medical report if requested. As with business records, arbitrators have power to admit medical reports, without requiring that the doctor who prepared the report be called as a witness, in the exercise of their discretion to accept evidence,

9 See *R. v. Khan*, [1990] 2 S.C.R. 531.
10 R.S.O. 1990, c.E.23, s.35. See Appendix 1.
11 R.S.O. 1990, c.E.23, s.52. See Appendix 1.

whether or not it is admissible in a court of law.

Although some arbitrators do not necessarily require that statutory rules as to notice be complied with, others expect advance notice to be given, so that the opposite party can consult its own medical experts, and decide whether to require that the doctor attend for cross-examination. The doctor's attendance should be required only where the medical report is unclear and requires further elaboration; if the doctor is required to give oral evidence unnecessarily, an award of costs may be made.[12]

Privilege

In Canada, witnesses cannot refuse to answer questions put to them on the ground that the answer may be incriminating, although their testimony may not be used against them in subsequent proceedings.[13] However, a witness has the right to refuse to disclose matters which are privileged. These include: settlement discussions; solicitor-client communications; documents prepared in anticipation of litigation; spousal exchanges; and matters protected by a relationship of confidence. Indeed, arbitrators have exercised their statutory discretion to exclude evidence, whether or not it is excluded by the courts, where there are sound labour relations reasons for doing so.[14] Thus, discussions during the grievance procedure are considered privileged, because the admission of such evidence would likely inhibit a full and frank exchange of views. This privilege does not, however, extend to statements made during an investigatory meeting prior to the imposition of discipline.

The Collateral Facts Rule

In Canada, cross-examination is not limited to areas of evidence addressed by the witness in chief; if the purpose of the questioning is to test credibility, cross-examination can be employed to probe collateral facts, i.e. facts which do not prove or disprove a matter in issue before the arbitrator. However, a party cannot contradict the answer given to a collateral question by calling evidence to rebut it; otherwise, the hearing would result in a series of mini-trials to determine side issues. Nonetheless, there are several exceptions to the rule against proof of collateral facts; these permit proof of a witness' prior inconsistent statements, criminal record, bias or partiality.

12 See *Municipality of Metropolitan Toronto* (1992), 25 L.A.C. (4th) 73 (Springate).
13 *Canada Evidence Act*, R.S.C. 1985, c.C-5; Ontario *Evidence Act*, R.S.O. 1990, c.E.23, s.9.
   See Appendix 1. See also s.13 of the *Canadian Charter of Rights and Freedoms*.
14 *Canada Post Corp.* (1993), 27 L.A.C. (4th) 178 (Swan).

Proof of Documents

Documents should be introduced through witnesses who can satisfy the arbitrator that they are what they purport to be. Documents can be authenticated by calling the writer, by calling a witness who saw the document being written or signed, by an admission from the party against whom the document is tendered, by comparison of the document with others established as genuine, by the testimony of a witness with general knowledge of the writer's handwriting, or by the testimony of a handwriting expert. Photographs, plans, maps, surveys and drawings can be proved by calling a witness to testify to the accuracy of the representation. In many cases, documents are admitted on the agreement of the parties. Even where there is no agreement, there is a tendency on the part of arbitrators to relax the strict requirements of technical proof, provided it is apparent that the document in question has been received by the witness. Once admitted, documents should be marked as exhibits, and photocopies should be made available as required.

The Best Evidence Rule

The best evidence rule provides that the original of a document should be introduced rather than a copy, unless the original is not available. It is common practice, however, to file photocopies on consent, and the rule itself has buckled under the weight of electronic systems of information processing.

The Rule Against Self-Serving Statements

According to this rule, prior consistent statements by a witness are not admissible because they are so easily manufactured. There are, however, three exceptions to the rule against self-serving statements: statements which were contemporaneous with the event in question; statements adduced in response to a charge of recent fabrication; and evidence of a recent complaint by a victim made shortly after a sexual or other attack.

Character Evidence

In a criminal proceeding, character evidence, i.e. evidence of the witness' general reputation in the community for honesty and integrity, is admissible to support the credibility of the accused, and as the basis of an inference that he or she is unlikely to have committed the offence. However, since the ordinary witness is assumed to be as honest as the next person, evidence as to good character cannot be called in a civil proceeding, such as an arbitration hearing, unless the witness' character has been attacked, or the witness' character itself is an issue in the case, as where honesty is a qualification required for promotion to a position of trust. The rule restricting character evidence should arguably be relaxed where criminal or quasi-criminal conduct is alleged in an arbitration proceeding. Moreover, in arbitration cases involving discipline or discharge, where the grievor's character is often relevant to the issue of penalty, the common law rules regarding character evidence are likely less applicable.

Similar Fact Evidence

In criminal cases, evidence of similar conduct in the past, i.e. similar fact evidence, may be admissible to show a disposition to commit certain misconduct, but only if the evidence sought to be introduced shows a sufficient connection between the act alleged and previous acts of misconduct, and the probative value of the proposed evidence outweighs its prejudicial effect. However, in civil proceedings such as arbitration, unless criminal or quasi-criminal conduct is alleged, evidence of similar facts will likely be admitted if it is relevant to prove an issue in the case, as long as it is not unduly oppressive or unfair to the other side.

Expert Evidence

Only an expert witness, who testifies on a matter within a particular area of expertise, can give opinion evidence. The Ontario courts require that the expert's report be served on the opposite party at least 10 days before trial.[15] Ordinary witnesses must confine their testimony to observations of fact, and cannot give opinions except as to common matters, such as the identity of people, their ages, emotional and physical state, the speed of vehicles, the distance of an object from the viewer and the physical condition of an object. Not all expert evidence is admissible. Thus, for example, the majority of arbitrators have refused to admit polygraph evidence, and the Supreme Court of Canada has condemned it. In general, however, the scope of expert evidence has been broadened by the courts, and it will no longer necessarily be considered inadmissible simply because it is based on information that is not presented as evidence, or because it may address the ultimate issue before the tribunal.

---

15 *Rules of Civil Procedure (Ontario Court of Justice)*, R.R.O. 1990, Reg. 194, s.53.03.

The Parole Evidence Rule

Extrinsic evidence, such as evidence of past practice or statements made during negotiations, is not admissible to vary the terms of a collective agreement, but it is admissible to resolve ambiguities, and to support an argument of estoppel, i.e. a claim that the opposite party should be precluded from insisting on the strict terms of the collective agreement because it has made a representation, upon which there has been detrimental reliance, that it would not do so.

Current Trends

A recent article on the law of evidence notes that "the most recent significant changes in the way we deal with the law of evidence have been a decrease in technicality and an increase in the use of general, discretionary, standards for the admission of proof".[16] These comments apply to the courts. One would expect arbitrators to be even more liberal in their approach to evidence, since they are not bound by the strict rules of evidence, and have a statutory discretion to accept evidence, whether or not it is admissible in a court of law. However, this is not necessarily the case. Indeed, the Ontario Court of Appeal has expressed a concern regarding "the extreme legal formalism and adherence to technical rules which overhangs the arbitration process", and has noted that "while it may be helpful for arbitration boards to seek guidance by way of analogy from established legal procedures, they risk committing jurisdictional error by rigid adherence to them".[17]

The tendency on the part of most arbitrators today, where a dispute arises, is to hear evidence that is arguably relevant, without ruling on admissibility, and to decide at the conclusion of the hearing how much weight to place upon the evidence.This approach is likely to be fortified by the Supreme Court of Canada's recent ruling in *Université du Québec* quashing an arbitration award where crucial evidence on an important point was disallowed.[18] In concurring reasons, Justice L'Heureux-Dubé stated that "the formalism and inflexibility demonstrated by the arbitrator in this case have no place in the hearing of a grievance. If the arbitrator had doubts as to the relevancy of the evidence sought to be introduced, he could have taken it under advisement as courts regularly do. This would have facilitated and speeded up the hearing".

16 David Paciocco, *"The Law of Evidence: Recasting Rules to Perform New Roles"*, in Special Lectures of the Law Society of Upper Canada, 1991 (Carswell, 1992) p.1.
17 *Re City of Toronto and Canadian Union of Public Employees, Local 79* (1982), 133 D.L.R. (3d) 94 (Ont.C.A.), *per* Blair J.A. at 108.
18 *Syndicat des employés professionels v. Université du Québec à Trois-Rivières* (1993), 101 D.L.R. (4th) 494 (S.C.C.). See Appendix 7.

CHAPTER 9

Examining Your Own Witness: Examination-In-Chief

The Purpose of Examination-in-Chief

The purpose of examining your own witness—referred to as examination-in-chief or direct examination—is to elicit evidence helpful to your case. You must decide in advance whether it is necessary or desirable to call a particular witness. In doing so, you should ask yourself whether the witness will make a good impression in chief and perform well under cross-examination. Since cross-examination is not limited to matters that are the subject of examination-in-chief, it is important to canvass with the witness in advance all relevant matters of which the witness has knowledge, in order to ensure that the witness does not possess information damaging to your case that could be extracted on cross-examination.

Leading Questions Restricted

Questioning a witness in chief must be conducted in accordance with the rules of evidence. Thus, you are not permitted to ask your own witness leading questions, i.e. questions which suggest the answer or assume a fact that is in dispute. In effect, by asking leading questions, you are giving the evidence yourself. For this reason, answers given to leading questions are usually given little weight, and there is not much point in asking them. Don't ask a grievor: "Did the supervisor provoke you by using abusive language?" Rather, ask: "Did the supervisor say anything to you before you walked off the job?" However, there are exceptions to this general rule. You can ask leading questions where they relate to introductory or non-essential facts, or in order to establish the context, or to elicit facts which are not in dispute. You can direct a witness to the incident in question if the witness forgets or the matter is complicated. If the witness leaves something out, you may be allowed to ask for further information.

In general, although you are not allowed to ask your own witness leading questions on matters in dispute, there is a discretion in the arbitrator, where it is necessary in the interests of justice, to permit it. Thus, if a witness has difficulty testifying accurately because of infirmity, age or immaturity, leading questions will be permitted. Again, where you call an unfriendly witness who is closely connected with the opposite party—such as the grievor if you represent the employer, or a supervisor if you represent the union—you may be allowed some latitude in asking leading questions, provided restraint is exercised, but arbitrators are divided as to whether to relax the rule in such cases.[19]

Refreshing the Witness' Memory Allowed

Despite the prohibition against leading questions, and a concern that documents will supplant testimony, you can refresh the witness' memory through contemporaneous documents, such as notes prepared by the witness at the time of the incident. In other words, once the witness' present recollection is exhausted, the witness will be allowed, if it is necessary, to use notes or documents as an *aide-memoire* to refresh his or her memory, but only if the notes were made at the time of the event in question or at a time when the witness could still be expected to recall the events accurately. If the notes were made by another, they can still be used, if the accuracy of the notes was verified at a time when the witness' memory was fresh. These notes do not automatically become evidence. However, they can be inspected by the opposite party, and filed as an exhibit during cross-examination.

This procedure, referred to as present memory refreshed, is to be distinguished from past recollection recorded. In the latter case, where a witness has no memory of the event, but the record is made as part of a work routine, or its accuracy can be confirmed, it can be used to refresh the witness' memory, regardless whether or not it is contemporaneous, but in these circumstances the record itself must be filed as an exhibit.

One must be careful about using previous testimony during examination-in-chief. You cannot simply relate to a witness his or her testimony from an earlier proceeding and ask if it is correct, nor

---

19 The *Rules of Civil Procedure (Ontario Court of Justice)* provide: Where a witness appears unwilling or unable to give responsive answers, the trial judge may permit the party calling the witness to examine him or her by means of leading questions. See R.R.O. 1990, Reg. 194, s.53.01(4).

can you advise a witness of the substance of the evidence of the previous witness and ask him or her to adopt it. On the other hand, you can put a statement to a witness, where another witness has testified that he or she made it, and ask the witness whether he or she denies doing so. First, however, you should ask the witness for his or her own recollection.

Be sure to review notes with the witness *before* you put him or her on the stand so that the witness does not become confused. If a witness reviews notes or documents, in order to refresh his or her memory prior to giving evidence, but they are not used to refresh the witness' memory during examination-in-chief, arbitrators are divided as to whether these notes or documents must be produced on cross-examination.

Cross-Examination Not Permitted Unless Witness Hostile

In general, if you call a witness, you vouch for that witness' credibility, and you cannot seek to discredit the witness through cross-examination, simply because you are not satisfied with the answer that has been given. However, if the witness is reluctant to tell the truth, or appears to be hostile or clearly opposed in interest, you may ask the arbitrator for permission to cross-examine. Also, where the witness has made a prior inconsistent statement, you can ask that the witness be declared adverse, and engage in cross-examination.[20] You should put the statement to the witness, but you can call evidence to prove the statement if the witness denies having made it.

This turn of events is obviously rare. Normally, you will not call a witness unless you are certain as to the evidence he or she will give. Moreover, unless the witness adopts the prior inconsistent statement as the true version of events, and is believed by the arbitrator, all that you will have accomplished is to nullify the credibility of a witness whom you yourself have called. Indeed, the arbitrator may still choose to believe the witness' testimony despite a contradictory statement. However, it does occasionally happen that a witness will change his or her story unexpectedly, and in such circumstances you may have no alternative but to seek to have the witness declared hostile.[21]

---

20 For procedure in civil actions, see section 9 of the *Canada Evidence Act*, R.S.C. 1985, c. C-5, and section 23 of the Ontario *Evidence Act*, R.S.O. 1990, c.E.23. See Appendix 1.
21 A recent decision of the Supreme Court of Canada reforms the rule which limits the use of prior inconsistent statements to impeaching the credibility of a witness; such statements can now be admitted as evidence if they are reliable and it is necessary to do so: see *R. v. B. (K.G.)*, unreported, February 25, 1993.

While the tendency of courts and arbitrators is to require witnesses to explain a change of story, the view prevails that parties ought not generally to be allowed to cross-examine their own witnesses, and prior inconsistent statements are not admitted indiscriminately. In most instances, the issue will not be of great importance, and you can call other witnesses who can clarify the matter, even if their evidence is contradictory. Sometimes, however, the matter will be of such importance that it is necessary to discredit a witness whom you yourself have called.

Hearsay Questions Limited

Witnesses must base their testimony on first-hand knowledge, and not hearsay. As discussed above, the rule against hearsay means that you should not ask a witness to report a statement made by someone else, who is not also called as a witness, if it is your intention to rely on the truth of the information contained in that statement. The reason for this rule is that the opposite party would be deprived of an opportunity to cross-examine the person who in fact made the statement. It is not hearsay, however, if you want to prove that the statement was made in order to establish notice or a statement of mind, and nothing turns on its truth. Again, affidavit evidence is not normally admissible, since it is not subject to cross-examination.

There are, however, exceptions to the rule against hearsay, such as admissions against interest, and it is on this basis that the grievor or other union witnesses may give evidence of statements made by representatives of the employer, and supervisors may report statements made by the grievor. While documents may constitute hearsay, unless introduced by the author who can be subject to cross-examination, exceptions are made in certain circumstances for such documents as business records and medical reports. See page 84.

Questions Must Be Relevant

The questions you ask must be relevant to the issues in dispute. However, not all relevant matters may be explored. As indicated, questions which elicit hearsay are restricted. So, too, are questions which relate to "privileged" matters, such as discussions during the grievance procedure. You cannot ask a witness about a prior consistent statement, unless recent fabrication is suggested, since this is considered to be self-serving.

Collateral Questions Not Allowed

Even though you may cross-examine the opposite party's witnesses on collateral or unrelated matters, for the purpose of testing credibility, you cannot ask your own witness questions which are designed to elicit contradictory testimony on such matters. Exceptions permit proof of a witness' prior inconsistent statements, criminal record, bias or partiality.

Opinion Evidence Limited

Ask your witness factual questions, and avoid questions which require an opinion unless the witness is qualified as an expert. A witness should be asked to give his or her observations, rather than conclusions. For example, a witness may testify that someone had glassy eyes, and gave off the odour of alcohol, but should not give an opinion as to whether the person was drunk. If your witness is an expert, you must qualify him as such, before asking for an opinion.

Handling Objections

If the opposing advocate objects to one of your questions, deal with the objection before proceeding with your question. In dealing with the objection, address your submissions to the arbitrator, not the opposing advocate. Examples of common objections to questions asked in chief are set out at the end of this chapter.

Taking Notes

It is not necessary to write down your questions verbatim. Instead, you may be better advised to list the points you want to cover under topical headings. This will enable you to concentrate on your witness rather than on your notes. Remember to indicate in your notes the points, during the witness' evidence, when you will want to introduce documents. Try to have someone who is with you transcribe the testimony which is given while you question the witness, since it is difficult to make notes yourself while you are asking questions. If no one else is available to take notes, you can often rely on the notes made by yourself in preparing the witness prior to the hearing, but you should record any testimony given by the witness which departs from the version of events which he or she gave you prior to the hearing. You will want to have accurate notes of the evidence in order to prepare final argument.

Give Your Witness Advice

Try to make your witness feel comfortable. Advise the witness to look the arbitrator in the eye, and to speak slowly enough so that the arbitrator can take notes, and firmly enough so that the arbitrator can hear. Witnesses should be cautioned not to nod in answer in questions, since a nod cannot be recorded. If a witness gives answers indicating physical distance or direction, these should be explained in words, rather than indicated by the witness through movements. You may be able to help the witness correct inappropriate habits of communication, such as responding to a question with a question. See Advice to Witnesses, at page 62. Guidelines respecting communications with witnesses giving evidence are set out at the end of the next chapter.

Spotlight the Witness

Introduce your witness with some personal details so as to bring out his or her personality. Then relate the witness to the case, and elicit his or her story. Ask the witness to focus his or her mind on the events in question. Then give the witness as much opportunity to tell the story in his or her own words. Stay in the background. The witness should dominate, the advocate remain unobtrusive. Do not interrupt excessively. Your questions should be short, the answers long. As much as possible, allow your witness to give narrative answers, but make sure that he or she does not leave out some vital detail. If he or she does, you will have to ask further questions, in a non-leading way, to draw out the additional information.

Focus on the Facts

Make sure that you prepare a foundation for the questions you ask. For example, before you ask a witness to give his or her observations, make sure that details are given regarding the circumstances in which the observations were made. Advise your witness in advance to testify as to facts, without giving an opinion, unless requested to do so. When stating facts, however, the witness should be firm, if he or she is certain, and not use vague language suggesting uncertainty, such as "I think" or "I believe" or "I guess". Instruct the witness to testify on the basis of personal knowledge, and avoid reporting statements made by others, unless advised that it is proper to do so.

Make Your Questions Clear and Interesting

Be clear and concise in your questions. Your questions should be straightforward, and you should use plain language. Ask one question at a time. Avoid compound or double-barrelled questions, i.e. questions which contain other questions within themselves. Do not repeat the answer. Try to make your questions interesting. Questions which relate to a particular topic engage one's attention more than a plodding process of chronological questioning. Attempt to look as if you have not heard the whole story before. You may do this by injecting a note of drama into your questioning, by showing an interest in the grievor's answers, or by focusing attention on the witness through an instruction to the witness to give a particular answer "slowly and carefully". Try to conclude your examination in chief on a high note that permits the witness, in effect, to summarize the thrust of his or her evidence.

Introducing Documents

Documents can be filed as evidence in their own right (so-called *real* evidence) if they are relevant, genuine, and verified by a witness. With permission of the arbitrator, they may be introduced before the witness who authenticates them gives evidence, in which case they will be marked for identification, and entered as an exhibit once they are authenticated by the appropriate witness. Documents can also be used as *demonstrative* evidence or aids to memory.

Make a list of documents which you intend to file as exhibits, and introduce those documents, if you can, through the person who prepared them or received them. Ask the witness to identify the signature and the nature of the document. This process of "authentication" is the method by which documents are properly introduced. In describing spatial arrangements and the movement of people, you may find it useful to have your witness draw a diagram, and mark the position of various people on it. This document can then be filed as an exhibit. Ordinarily, the arbitrator will mark each exhibit with an identifying number or letter. You should mark your copies of the exhibits, using the same numbering system, and keep a list of the exhibits in the order in which they have been filed. You will need them for cross-examination and for argument.

In certain circumstances, business records and medical reports may be introduced in civil proceedings without calling the persons who prepared them, provided that notice is given to the opposite party in advance of the hearing.[22] If proper notice has not been given, in accordance with statutory requirements, the arbitrator has a discretion to admit such evidence, whether or not it is admissible in a court of law. Of course, you may call the physician who prepared the medical report, or the clerk who drew up the business records, to testify regarding them. It is advisable to file the best evidence, e.g. original documents with signatures, unless they are not available, although the best evidence rule has been relaxed as a result of technological advances in the transfer of information.

Examples of common objections to the introduction of documents are set out at the end of this chapter.

Questioning Your Expert Witness

When you call an expert as a witness, you must first qualify the witness as an expert. You should elicit from the expert his or her current profession, academic credentials, work experience, professional associations, scholarly publications, and other unique credentials. You should ask the expert to explain his or her specialty, and set out the factual basis of his or her opinion, and the assumptions upon which it is based. The expert should then be asked to give his or her opinion, and review other opinions, if that is appropriate.

Failing to Call a Material Witness

Remember that, if you fail to call a material witness, the opposing advocate may ask the arbitrator to draw the inference that his or her evidence would have been unfavourable to your case. Of course, you may do the same if the opposing advocate fails to call a material witness during the presentation of the opposite party's case.

One Last Word

Never, never call a witness without reviewing his or her evidence in advance with that witness.

---

22 Ontario *Evidence Act*, R.S.O. 1990, c. E.23, ss. 35, 52. See Appendix 1.

COMMON OBJECTIONS TO
QUESTIONS ASKED IN CHIEF

☐ The question relates to an irrelevant issue.

☐ The question is leading, in that it hints at or suggests the answer, or assumes a fact that has not been proved. The question lacks a proper foundation because it presumes a background of fact which has not been established. The advocate is giving evidence, through the question, rather than the witness.

☐ The question involves cross-examination of the advocate's own witness. For example, it challenges the witness' credibility, although the witness has not been shown to be hostile or adverse simply because the witness has given an answer that is unfavourable to the advocate's cause.

☐ The question invites a hearsay answer, or the answer contains hearsay, rather than a statement of facts based on personal knowledge.

☐ The question calls for, or the answer contains, an opinion, although the witness has not been qualified as an expert.

☐ The question calls for speculation or a hypothetical answer, rather than facts.

☐ The question invites a legal opinion regarding interpretation of the collective agreement, and this is a matter for the arbitrator to decide.

☐ The question relates to a "privileged matter", such as discussions during the grievance procedure.

☐ The question relates to past practice or statements made during negotiations, and is asked for the purpose of determining the meaning of the collective agreement, although this is permitted only where the agreement is ambiguous or an estoppel is asserted.

☐ The question is designed to elicit, or the answer given amounts to, self-serving evidence, such as a prior consistent statement.

☐ The question contains a misstatement of evidence that has previously been given.

☐ The question involves several questions which cannot be answered at the same time, i.e. it is a compound question.

☐ The question is designed to elicit answers that contradict the testimony given by witnesses for the opposite party, although such testimony dealt only with collateral matters, i.e. matters unrelated to the issues in dispute.

☐ The question invites evidence that would contradict the testimony given by a witness for the opposite party, although the matter was not put to that witness on cross-examination, so that he or she had no opportunity to explain.

COMMON OBJECTIONS TO
THE INTRODUCTION OF DOCUMENTS

☐ The document is not relevant to the issues in dispute.

☐ The document contains hearsay, since the author is not available for cross-examination, and it does not fit within permitted exceptions, such as business records and medical reports.

☐ The document is not the best evidence, in that it is not the original, when the original should be available.

☐ The document has not been properly introduced, i.e. the signature has not been identified and the nature of the document has not been described.

☐ The document has not been properly proved by a witness who can testify as to the circumstances in which it originated, or in which it was received.

☐ The document is being used without a proper foundation, e.g. to refresh a witness' memory although (1) it has not been established that it was prepared when the events were fresh in the witness' mind, (2) the document is inadmissible and cannot be used at all, or (3) the document is being shown to the witness but not offered in evidence.

CHAPTER 10

Cross-Examination

The Purpose of Cross-Examination

The purpose of cross-examination is to elicit favourable testimony and undermine unfavourable testimony. This can be done by attacking the evidence directly or by discrediting the witness.

The scope of cross-examination is very broad. You can ask leading questions, suggest the answers, if you want, and repeat questions in several ways. You are not confined in your questioning to areas covered by the witness in chief, and you may ask questions regarding collateral or unrelated issues, if they are designed to test the witness' credibility. Although you may not be unduly abusive or insulting, tedious or repetitive, you are entitled to a full opportunity to test the witness' evidence and the witness' veracity. However, you must conduct your cross-examination fairly and in accordance with the rules of evidence.[23]

The arbitrator cannot join the fray by taking over cross-examination, nor should he or she interrupt the flow of questioning or limit the length of time an advocate takes in cross-examination. Rather, the arbitrator should rule on the propriety of the evidence, question by question, and curtail further questioning only if full opportunity has been given for cross-examination, and the questioning has become tedious or vexatious.

Should You Cross-Examine?

You have a right to cross-examine, but you have no obligation to do so. If the witness has said nothing that damages your case, there may be no point in conducting a cross-examination, unless you believe

---

23 The *Rules of Civil Procedure (Ontario Court of Justice)* provide: The trial judge shall exercise reasonable control over the mode of interrogation of a witness so as to protect the witness from undue harassment or embarrassment and may disallow a question put to a witness that is vexatious or irrelevant to any matter that may properly be inquired into at the trial. R.R.O. 1990, Reg. 194, s.53.01(2).

that you can elicit helpful testimony. However, while most cases are decided on the basis of the clash of opposing witnesses, cross-examination can be crucial, especially where credibility is involved. Indeed, if there is a failure to cross-examine, in circumstances where it is reasonable to expect it, the failure to do so will enhance the credibility of the witness. If you decide to cross-examine, do not feel that you have to question a witness regarding each and every matter upon which the witness has given evidence. Much of the witness' testimony may not have been damaging to your case, and may not require to be pursued on cross-examination. On the other hand, you can cross-examine regarding matters that have not been addressed by the witness in chief.

Preparing Cross-Examination

Cross-examination should be carefully thought out in advance. You will have given some thought to the witnesses you expect the opposing advocate will call before the hearing begins, and you will have prepared some questions for cross-examination, based on your knowledge of the case. Do not write down your questions verbatim, but rather note the points you wish to cover. In this way, you can concentrate on the witness rather than on your notes. But your first opportunity to actually observe the opposite party's witnesses usually occurs only when they take the stand. You must pay careful attention as they give evidence, and listen attentively to their testimony, not solely for the purpose of raising objections to improper questions, but also for the purpose of considering the implications of their evidence for the entire case, and of ascertaining possible avenues for fruitful cross-examination. Pick out the weak spots in the witness' evidence and zero in on them.

Watch the witness closely during examination-in-chief for any signs of uncertainty. Pauses or hesitations may signify that the witness knows more than he or she cares to reveal. This is your chance to take a measure of the witness' personality, and to decide on the approach you wish to employ in cross-examination. You should be in a position to take careful notes as the opposite party's witnesses give their evidence in chief. Indicate in the margin the answers you wish to explore further in cross-examination.

In preparing cross-examination, divide your notebook into three columns: the first for questions, arranged by topic or other logical method, the second for documents, exhibits and references to other evidence, and the third for the witness' answers. You should record the essence of the witness' answers as the witness testifies, if a colleague is not able to take verbatim notes. Underline the crucial admissions you will want to quote in final argument. Usually, only four or five phrases or documents are important. If it is your witness who is under cross-examination, take verbatim notes.

Dealing With Documents

You should have relevant documents at hand, with copies for the arbitrator and your adversary, and they should be arranged in the order in which you intend to use them, so that your cross-examination is not interrupted by a search for relevant material. Remember that you may be able to introduce additional documents, which you have not been able to authenticate through your own witnesses, by putting them to the opposite party's witnesses on cross-examination. Mark exhibits clearly with an identifying number.

Engage the Witness

When you question a witness, make sure the witness faces you, and not his or her own advocate. Otherwise, the witness may look to the opposite advocate for encouragement or even signals as to how to respond. Remember that the arbitrator is usually in a position to see everyone in the hearing room. You should therefore advise members of your party not to react, verbally or visibly, to testimony that is given.

Pay Attention to the Arbitrator

Be sure that the arbitrator has an opportunity to write down your questions and the witness' answer before proceeding to the next question. Do not lose the attention of the arbitrator.

Taking Notes

It is difficult for you to make your own notes of what the witness says while you are cross-examining. Ask one of your colleagues to take notes, but note down important admissions yourself. You will be able to take careful notes as the opposite party's witnesses give their evidence in chief. Indicate in the margin the answers you wish to explore further in cross-examination.

Discrediting the Witness

In cross-examination, you are not bound to accept the witness' answers. You are entitled to test them by further questioning, and to bring out inconsistencies. You can discredit a witness by putting to the witness: contradictions in his or her own testimony; conflicts with the testimony of others; prior inconsistent statements; questions testing the witness' memory, perception, judgment, and opportunities of observation; questions bearing on the witness' motivation, objectivity, character and credibility; and previous criminal convictions, if any.

Attempt to bring out a motive that would explain the self-interest of the witness in giving the answer that he or she has given so that you can later contend that he or she is biased, partial, or lacking in objectivity. However, be careful in attacking character, since if you fail, you may shore up the witness' credibility. Moreover, be cautious in suggesting directly to a witness that he or she is lying. The witness will probably only deny it.

If you are testing the reliability of a witness' recollection of an event, you may explore the mental state and opportunities for observation of the witness, a well as his or her powers of recall. For example, you may ask him or her whether he or she has a clear recollection, how it is that his or her recollection is so clear on one point, but not on another, whether he or she was in a position to see and hear what occurred, why it is that he or she was paying so much attention, whether he or she made notes of the event in question, whether his or her ability to observe was affected by anything relating to his or her own condition (e.g. eyesight, hearing) or to external circumstances (e.g. bad weather, darkness). In short, if you cannot attack a witness' honesty by suggesting improper motive, you may be able to undermine the reliability of his or her evidence by suggesting poor memory or impaired perception.

Turning Witnesses to Your Advantage

Remember that you are not restricted in cross-examination to asking questions only about areas which the witness has covered in chief. You are free to ask the witness questions about any matter that is relevant to the issues, or about collateral or unrelated matters, if the questioning is for the purpose of testing the witness' credibility. Remember that it may be in your interest to ask a witness questions not only regarding what he or she has said, but what he or she has left out, or not said. Consider asking about other areas of which the witness may have knowledge, and probe these areas to determine whether you can elicit helpful testimony. Test the witness, for example, by asking him or her about conversations he or she may have had with other witnesses regarding the events in question. Often, the witness will not have been prepared for this approach, and may disclose evidence valuable to your cause. By this means, you can occasionally turn a witness to your advantage.

Collateral Questions As to Credibility

In order to test a witness' credibility, you may question the witness regarding matters which are not relevant to the issues in dispute. If the witness is seen to be untruthful regarding these collateral issues, you can argue that the witness' evidence as a whole cannot be relied upon. However, in order to prevent a series of mini-trials into the truth or untruth of unrelated collateral issues, you will not be permitted to call evidence to contradict the witness' answers on these points. This does not mean that the witness' answers have to be accepted as the truth. Moreover, you are entitled to probe the witness' answers, but you cannot call contradictory evidence if the witness insists on giving the same answer. There are exceptions to the rule against calling evidence on collateral issues. You can, for example, call evidence relating to the witness' bad character, lack of credibility, and any mental defect rendering the witness incapable of belief.

Cross-Examining on Notes Used to Refresh Memory

You can, if you wish, ask a witness to produce any notes or documents, whether or not authored by the witness, which are used to refresh the witness' memory *while* testifying, whether or not the notes or documents are otherwise protected by privilege. Then, you can cross-examine on those parts of it that relate to the issues in the case, in order to show inconsistencies with the witness' testimony. You can mark the notes or documents as exhibits. If it becomes apparent that the witness has used notes or documents to refresh his or her memory, *before* giving evidence, it is for the arbitrator to decide whether such notes or documents must be produced. It can be argued that they should be produced in order to test whether the witness' recollection is accurate. An attempt should be made to extract from the witness any notes in his or her possession, contemporaneous with the incident, that may be relevant to the issues.

Raising Prior Inconsistent Statements

One of the most effective methods of cross-examination is to confront a witness with a prior inconsistent statement. The purpose of this type of cross-examination is to show that the witness should not be believed as he or she told a different story on other occasions. For this purpose, it is important to obtain prior statements of a witness, preferably before the hearing begins. Such statements can be used to discredit the witness. Indeed, evidence of prior inconsistent statements of a witness other than an accused may now be substantively admissible if the necessity arises and the evidence is reliable: see *R. v. B. (K.G.)*, footnote 21 at page 91.

However, before you confront a witness with a prior inconsistent statement, you should set the hook by committing the witness to his or her testimony before proceeding to contrast it with the prior statement. First, ask the witness whether or not he or she wishes to affirm or change the evidence he or she has given. Then, ask the witness if he or she made a prior statement, giving particulars of the date and circumstances. If the prior statement is admitted, you may cross-examine upon it. If the witness denies making such a statement, you may show the witness the statement. If the witness continues to deny having made the statement, you may call another witness to prove that it was made, although this would ordinarily be done as part of your own case.[24] Whether the entire statement should be marked as an exhibit is within the discretion of the arbitrator. For this reason, before raising a prior inconsistent statement, you should weigh the advantage of contradicting the witness against the effect of the disclosure of other matters in the statement that might be prejudicial to your case.

Cross-Examining About Criminal Record

You can cross-examine about a previous criminal conviction, or other criminal misconduct, on the basis that this is a matter going to credibility, either under common law or pursuant to statute.[25] If the conviction is denied, you can prove it by producing a certificate. However, the impact of this evidence on the witness' credibility may be limited, especially where the witness acknowledges his or her record when giving evidence in chief.

Give the Witness A Chance to Explain

If you intend to discredit a witness by calling evidence to contradict the witness' version of facts, then you must put to the witness the substance of the contradictory evidence you propose to adduce, and

24 *Canada Evidence Act*, R.S.C. 1985, c.C-5, s.10; Ontario *Evidence Act*, R.S.O. 1990, c.E.23, s.20. See Appendix 1.
25 *Canada Evidence Act*, s.12; Ontario *Evidence Act*, s.22. See Appendix 1.

give the witness a fair opportunity to explain his or her position. You might introduce the question by stating: "I will be calling witness X who will say the following—what do you have to say to that?" It would be unfair to fail to challenge a witness' evidence in cross-examination, and then to ask the arbitrator to disbelieve what the witness has said, although not one question was directed either to the witness' credibility or to the accuracy of the witness' testimony. This rule, laid down by the English House of Lords in *Browne v. Dunn*,[26] and followed by courts and tribunals in Canada, is designed to accord fairness to witnesses and to the parties.

The rule does not apply where the evidence is introduced for purposes other than impeaching credibility, e.g. simply to add details of conversations raising no adverse implications regarding credibility. Moreover, the rule is not absolute, and may be relaxed, for example, where the testimony is of such a nature that it is obvious that credibility is in issue. There is also a discretion to allow such evidence, even though the contradictory version of events was not put to the witness when he or she initially gave evidence, if the witness has an opportunity to dispute that version by giving evidence in reply. However, the discretion is exercised sparingly because the witness, if called in reply, would be subject to further cross-examination.

Don't Suggest Misconduct You Can't Prove

While you cannot give evidence yourself, you can suggest that the facts are such and so and ask the witness to confirm or deny it. However, it is dangerous to suggest misconduct that you cannot prove, and you should not suggest facts if there is no reasonable basis in the evidence, or if you have no information or material in your possession which would give rise to a reasonable belief that they are true.

Querying the Failure to Call a Witness

If you intend to argue, at the conclusion of the hearing, that an adverse inference should be drawn against the opposite party, because of its failure to call a particular witness, you should lay the groundwork by asking questions of other witnesses that underline the absent witness' material role in events, and confirm that the witness is either present in the hearing room, or available to be called as a witness.

26 (1893), 6 R. 67 (H.L.).

Can You Cross-Examine a "Friendly" Witness?

Where the opposite party has called a witness who is friendly to your cause, i.e. with a natural bias in favour of your case, you may not be permitted to ask leading questions, or cross-examine. If you are permitted to cross-examine, in such circumstances, the arbitrator may warn that little weight will be given to answers to leading questions. It is better practice to question such a witness as if you were examining him or her in chief.

Hearsay Questions Limited

You cannot ask questions which are likely to result in the introduction of inadmissible evidence, such as questions which call for information based, not on personal knowledge, but on hearsay. If you do, and the opposing advocate does not object, you run the risk that the person who gave the information may not be called as a witness, and you will have lost your opportunity to cross-examine that person.

Opinion Evidence Restricted

You may not ask questions that invite opinions, unless the witness is qualified as an expert. Your questions should be confined to the facts. You should not ask a witness legal questions, or debate points of law.

Privileged Matters Out of Bounds

You may not ask questions about privileged matters, such as discussions during the grievance procedure.

Questioning Must Be Directed

In deciding which path to follow in cross-examination, you must have a game plan. All your questions must be consistent with your theory of the case. Every question should be directed to a specific purpose. Random, aimless questioning will only lead you into blind alleys. Try to ask questions that require a "yes" or "no" answer, i.e. closed questions. Open-ended questions, such as "what happened?", allow the witness to advance his or her own case or explain away his or her conduct. If the opposing advocate argues that you are cutting off the witness, respond by noting that the witness will have an opportunity to explain his or her answers on re-examination. At all times, you must be in control. Try to frame questions in such a way that the witness has no option other than to give you the information you seek, and preferably with a "yes" or "no" answer. Don't ramble. All questions should be directed to a specific goal, calculated to extract a particular expected response. There is no room for aimless interrogation.

Avoid Open-Ended Questions

Be careful about open-ended questions since they may allow the witness to supply information favourable to his or her position. Avoid questions that give an opportunity to explain, such as questions beginning: "Why?" or "What do you mean?" or "Why do you say that?" or "What happened?" or "How could you have seen that?" You should probe critical areas, where a witness may give a damaging answer, gingerly, on a step-by-step basis, so that you can retreat quickly, if need be, before any damage is done. The questions must be controlled, directed to producing certain answers. Do not disclose the purpose of your questioning. Otherwise, the witness may be evasive.

Step By Step Questioning

Your questions should be focused on a particular point. The witness should not be given an opportunity to give expansive answers. If the witness persists in doing so, ask the witness to inform you if he or she cannot answer "yes" or "no" to a specific question, and then rephrase the question. You cannot insist on a "yes" or "no" answer, but you can insist on an answer that is responsive to your question. Repeat the question if necessary. If the witness is evasive, you may ask the arbitrator to direct the witness to be responsive to your questions.

Closing the Escape Hatches

Before you pose a direct question on a critical matter, try to close the escape hatches by asking a series of preliminary questions so that, when you spring the trap, the witness cannot explain away his or her conduct. Avoid signalling or telegraphing the purpose of your questions since, if you do so, the witness will contrive to prepare an escape.

Don't "Retravel Direct"!

Do not "retravel direct". In other words, do not repeat to the witness, one by one, the answers that he or she has given on his or her examination-in-chief, with the suggestion that he or she is lying. By doing so, you will succeed only in giving the witness an opportunity to reiterate his or her earlier answers, but with greater emphasis. On the other hand, once a witness has made an admission, do not repeat the question in case the witness uses the opportunity to water down the answer. However, if the witness gives an answer that is damaging to your case, you may later want to approach the same subject matter, through a different set of questions, in order to lessen the damage.

Unsettling the Witness

It is not necessary to follow the order in which the witness gave evidence in chief or to pursue questions in a logical or chronological sequence. An orderly approach will allow the witness to consider his or her answers more carefully. You may shuffle the cards, and switch topics, change your pace and vary the tone of your voice, focus intensely upon a particular topic, or zig zag randomly from subject to subject, with a view to unsettling the witness. You may also speed up the pace of questions and answers so that the witness has less time to develop guarded responses. You can also take your time, even leave silences. Think over the witness' previous answers, as you proceed with your questioning, in order to determine whether there are inconsistencies that ought to be probed.

Questioning—Friendly or Aggressive?

Depending upon the witness, you may want to approach cross-examination in a friendly, rather than an aggressive, manner, on the theory that one can catch more flies with honey than with vinegar. Using this approach, you would begin your cross-examination by framing questions with a view toward maximizing agreement by the witness. Your tone should be matter of fact, not accusatory, for gentle questioning will ally fear, and disarm defiance. You may even smile encouragingly, and ask the witness to "help me out here". Often, witnesses are anxious to please, and to be accommodating, and you can promote this attitude by giving the witness the impression that you expect him or her to answer fairly. If the witness is evasive or defensive, you can become sharper in your questioning.

On the other hand, if you cannot gain the witness' confidence, it may be as well to try to unnerve him or her, right at the outset, by shaking the witness on a point that you are confident you can successfully establish. The advantage of this approach, if you succeed, is that you will sow doubt in the mind of the arbitrator regarding the rest of the testimony that the witness has given.

Your approach must be tailored to the witness. With decent, honest witnesses, there is no need to be abrasive. Indeed, harassing a mild-mannered witness will only win the witness the sympathy of the arbitrator. If the witness is belligerent, the arbitrator will likely conclude that the witness can take care of himself or herself, and you can afford to be firm.

Don't Go Too Far

Avoid asking a question to which you don't know the answer, if the wrong answer could damage your case, unless you have nothing to lose, since your case is otherwise a lost cause anyway. And be careful not to ask one question too many. Stop at the right point. If you obtain an admission that is helpful to your case and damaging to your opponent, avoid the temptation to gild the lily. You may undo all the good you have done.

Driving the Witness to Extremes

If the witness proves to be unyielding, and prepared to go to any extreme to oppose your case, it may occasionally be an effective tactic to allow the witness to make more and more exaggerated statements, so that at the end you can paint the witness' testimony as either unreasonable or incredible.

Suggesting the Opposite

Sometimes, if a witness is contrary or querulous, you may want to suggest the opposite of the answer you really wish, so that the witness will not know where you are going.

Dialogue with the Witness

A very effective method of cross-examination is to retrace with the witness his or her course of reasoning; the witness may become so involved in the dialogue that matters are revealed that would otherwise have been concealed.

Make it Clear and Simple

Do not ask compound or double-barrelled questions which contain several questions within themselves, since it will not be clear which question the witness is answering. Use simple language, and make your questions short and intelligible. Wait until the witness has answered one question before you ask another. But don't rush through a series of prepared questions. Listen to the answers that are given in case you wish to pursue them further with additional questions. Even if the witness' answers are off topic, it may be useful to follow them up at the time, rather than leaving them for later, when the witness may not be so forthcoming.

Don't React

Do not allow yourself to become excited or angry in questioning a witness, unless it is intentional. If the witness should become angry, it is even more important that you remain cool. Do not show surprise, disappointment or defeat. The arbitrator will notice it if you do. Act as if you expected each answer that is given.

Don't be Argumentative

Avoid being argumentative by presenting your own views in the course of questioning. Asking questions beginning: "Isn't it a fact that...?" or "I suggest that...", or "Isn't it true that...?" tend to invite denials, and can end up being argumentative. Do not try to get the witness to admit he or she is a liar. It won't work. Most witnesses don't lie, they just shade the truth. Occasionally, in questioning, you may wish to make a point, so that the arbitrator will know where you are headed, but on the whole you should avoid mixing argument with evidence. It will only alert the witness and the opposing advocate to where you are going, so that one can evade and the other prepare a response. The time to pull the threads of your evidence together is during final argument.

Asking About Witness Preparation

It may be useful to ask a witness whether he or she has discussed the matter in advance of the hearing with other witnesses or with his or her advocate in the presence of other witnesses, so that you can determine whether evidence has been influenced or fabricated. You may also inquire whether the witness has refreshed his or her memory prior to giving evidence by consulting notes or documents; in such a case, you should request that they be produced.

Dealing with Obstructive Tactics

Do not permit the witness to sit in a position where his or her advocate is in the witness' line of sight. The witness should be facing you, and not be able to seek help from his or her advocate or others in the room. Watch the opposing advocate to make sure that he or she does not signal to the witness what answers to give by nods of the head. If he or she does this, protest to the arbitrator that the opposing advocate is assisting the witness. If your questioning reaches a critical point, and the opposing advocate interjects in an effort to distract attention, or to give the witness time to think, or to suggest an answer, demand that the witness be excluded and point out to the arbitrator the stratagem of the opposing advocate.

Object to the opposing advocate's conduct as an attempt to interfere with legitimate questioning, and ask the arbitrator to direct the opposing advocate not to disrupt your cross-examination. Even if the arbitrator does not respond to your request, this will have a dampening effect on the readiness of the opposing advocate to interrupt you further. Where the opposing advocate makes an objection, and then launches into an argument that may indicate to the witness what answers he or she might give, you should move to block this tactic by requesting that the witness be excluded while the argument proceeds. When a ruling is given on the propriety of the question, the witness can then be asked to return to the hearing room. Examples of common objections to questions asked on cross-examination are set out at the end of this chapter.

Cross-Examining the Expert

If the witness is an expert, you may seek to challenge his or her qualifications. If that approach is not fruitful, you can question the facts on which the opinion is based, or the theory on which the opinion rests. Confront the witness with the views of other experts or authorities who hold contrary opinions.

Caution the Witness

If there is a break in the proceedings during cross-examination, ask the arbitrator to remind the witness that he or she may not discuss the case with anyone during cross-examination, including his or her own advocate. Detail one of your own party to keep an eye on the witness. You are entitled to ask the witness, when the hearing resumes, if he or she has discussed the matter with anyone during the recess, and what was said. If witnesses are excluded, arbitrators generally caution witnesses that they must not discuss their evidence with others, before all the evidence is concluded. Guidelines respecting communications with witnesses giving evidence are set out at the end of this chapter.

A Final Note

Close your cross-examination on a strong note, with a question that drives home the point of your case. End with a bang, not a whimper.

COMMON OBJECTIONS TO QUESTIONS
ASKED ON CROSS-EXAMINATION

☐ The question is irrelevant to the issues, and is not designed to test the witness' credibility.

☐ The question invites a hearsay answer, and does not fit within the exceptions to the rule against hearsay, which include admissions, declarations against interest, statements regarding mental or physical state, business documents and medical records, testimony from previous proceedings, and contemporaneous statements *(res gestae)*.

☐ The question relates to privileged matters, such as discussions during the grievance procedure.

☐ The question calls for an opinion, although the witness is not qualified as an expert.

☐ The question calls for speculation or a hypothetical answer, rather than facts.

☐ The question lacks a foundation in that it suggests facts which have not yet been proved in evidence.

☐ The question suggests misconduct, although the advocate asking the question has no evidence to support it.

☐ The question includes a misstatement of previous testimony.

☐ The questioning is unduly harsh and oppressive, and is designed to bully or badger, demean or ridicule.

☐ The question is confusing, or it includes several questions which cannot be answered at the same time, i.e. it is a compound or double-barrelled question.

☐ The question relates to past practice or statements made during negotiations, and is asked for the purpose of determining the meaning of the collective agreement, although this is permitted only where the agreement is ambiguous or an argument of estoppel is asserted.

☐ The question calls for a legal opinion, e.g. an interpretation of the contract, which is a matter for the arbitrator to decide.

Note: It is advisable to object only when it serves a purpose to do so. It makes little sense to object, even if the question is arguably improper, if no harm is done to your case by the witness' answer. When you do object, address the arbitrator, not the opposing advocate, and give your reasons for the objection.

COMMUNICATING WITH
WITNESSES GIVING EVIDENCE

The Rules of Professional Conduct governing Ontario lawyers, issued by the Law Society of Upper Canada, are a useful guide. They set out the following guidelines respecting communications with witnesses giving evidence:

(a) During examination-in-chief it is not improper for the examining lawyer to discuss with the witness any matter that has not been covered in the examination up to that point.

(b) During examination-in-chief by another lawyer of a witness who is unsympathetic to the lawyer's cause the lawyer not conducting the examination-in-chief may properly discuss the evidence with the witness.

(c) Between completion of examination-in-chief and commencement of cross-examination of the lawyer's own witness there ought to be no discussion of the evidence given in chief or relating to any matter introduced or touched upon during the examination-in-chief.

(d) During cross-examination by an opposing lawyer: While the witness is under cross-examination the lawyer ought not to have any conversation with the witness respecting the witness's evidence or relative to any issue in the proceeding.

(e) Between completion of cross-examination and commencement of re-examination the lawyer who is going to re-examine the witness ought not to have any discussion respecting evidence that will be dealt with on re-examination.

(f) During cross-examination by the lawyer of a witness unsympathetic to the cross-examiner's cause the lawyer may properly discuss the witness's evidence with the witness.

(g) During cross-examination by the lawyer of a witness who is sympathetic to that lawyer's cause any conversations ought to be restricted in the same way as communications during examination-in-chief of one's own witness.

(h) During re-examination of a witness called by an opposing lawyer: If the witness is sympathetic to the lawyer's cause there ought to be no communication relating to the evidence to be given by that witness during re-examination. The lawyer may, however, properly discuss the evidence with a witness who is adverse in interest.

If there is any question whether behaviour may be improper, the advocate is advised to obtain the consent of the opposing advocate and leave of the arbitrator before engaging in conversations that may be considered unethical. Such a situation may arise, for example, where a lengthy cross-examination raises new issues, and the only way to bring matters before the arbitrator in an orderly way is to discuss the evidence with the witness before re-examination.

CHAPTER 11

Re-Examination

The Purpose of Re-Examination

The purpose of re-examination is to explore, clarify and explain new matters raised in cross-examination. Hence, once your witness has been cross-examined by the opposing advocate, you can question the witness again, but only to address new matters arising out of the cross-examination, or to clarify, put matters in context, or explain a motive for an action referred to in cross-examination. If the rules are relaxed, and entirely new matters are raised in re-examination, further cross-examination will usually be permitted by the arbitrator.

The Technique of Re-Examination

Re-examination should be to the point. You should introduce your questions by referring to the witness' answer to a particular question on cross-examination, and ask the witness to clarify or explain. If the witness was permitted to respond only "yes" or "no" on cross-examination, you may use re-examination to bring out the rest of the story. The witness can give the answers he or she was prevented from giving. If the witness has given answers in chief that are inconsistent with answers given on cross-examination, you can ask questions on re-examination to clear up the confusion. However, do not re-examine on a point if you are not sure what the witness' answer will be. You may just make matters worse. It is difficult to rehabilitate a witness who has been badly shaken on cross-examination.

Objecting to Re-Examination

Generally speaking, the rules relating to re-examination are the same as those applicable to examination in chief. Thus, you are not allowed to ask leading questions of your own witness on re-examination any more than you could in chief. Objections that can be raised are also largely the same, although further objections may be made where a question posed in re-examination goes over the same ground that was covered in chief, or does not arise out of something that was raised for the first time in cross-examination.

CHAPTER 12

Presenting
Final Argument

The Nature of Argument

An argument is a summation of the evidence, the contract and the law as they relate to the issue in dispute. It is directed toward persuading the arbitrator of a particular conclusion, e.g. that the contract has been breached, and of the necessity for the granting of certain remedies, e.g. reinstatement with back pay in the case of discharge without just cause.

The Order of Presentation

The order of presenting argument depends upon who bears the burden of proof. In discharge or discipline cases, since the employer bears the burden of proof, the employer's advocate will normally go first, the union advocate will present rebuttal, and the employer's advocate will have a right of reply. In other cases, the order is reversed.

The Essential Elements

You should begin your argument by advising the arbitrator that you will proceed to deal with matters in the following order:
   (1) the issue or issues;
   (2) the applicable provisions of the collective agreement;
   (3) legal principles;
   (4) the evidence as it relates to the issues;
   (5) relevant authorities (texts, awards, legislation);
   (6) remedies requested.
   The order in which you address these topics is not immutable. Depending on the case, you may want to discuss the relevant principles of arbitration law at the same time as you analyze the authorities in detail. However, the advantage of dealing with general principles first, with a discussion of how they apply to the facts, is

that you are able to present your theory of the case, your rationale of the contract interpretation, and your submissions as to the facts, without becoming bogged down in case references. Once you construct the framework of the house, you can add to it, brick by brick.

The Manner of Presentation

The presentation of final argument does not require a rhetorical approach. You should speak with emphasis, but there is no need to raise your voice. This is not a jury address. The process involved in persuading an arbitrator is much more a dialogue than a debate. As a result, you should keep your eye on the arbitrator. Speak at a pace that will enable the arbitrator to make notes of what you say. Avoid the tendency to speed up, or rush through, your presentation. Remember that the outcome of the case will depend on the extent to which the arbitrator has confidence in your review of the facts and the law. It is important, therefore, to be balanced in your presentation of the facts, and to avoid extreme positions in outlining relevant legal principles.

It is also essential that you be alert to detect, and ready to address, the concerns of the arbitrator. For this reason, you should welcome any questions the arbitrator may ask, because these will give you an indication of what he or she is thinking. If you cannot answer immediately, indicate that you would like to consider the question further before responding or, if such is the case, that you will be coming to the point later in your argument. At the end of your argument, ask the arbitrator if he or she has any further questions to ask you, or whether you can be of any further assistance.

Do not write out your argument verbatim in advance of the hearing. Instead, prepare an outline of the points you wish to cover. This will enable you to think on your feet, to direct your attention to the arbitrator rather than to your notes, and to retain flexibility so that you can accommodate your argument to any unexpected turns that the evidence may have taken. Do not persist in an argument which has been prepared in advance if the evidence given at the hearing clearly does not support it. In short, be prepared to revise the content of your argument in light of the evidence that has been given.

Again, because the evidence may not turn out as you expect, and the nature of the issues may alter as you proceed, it is generally not advisable to file a written brief with the arbitrator, although it is desirable to prepare one for your own use. The situation is, of course, different if a direction is given, because of lack of time, to submit written argument following the hearing. In this case, you will have full opportunity to consider the evidence, and the issues, before filing your written brief.

When the opposing advocate presents argument, make a note of the principal points in his or her submissions, and leave a margin so that you can make notes of arguments to raise in response when your turn arrives to argue the case.

The Issues

When you set out the issues, it is important to do so with care and clarity. The way in which the issues are framed will significantly affect the outcome of the case. For example, is the issue whether the grievor quit, or whether he or she was discharged for just cause? Is the issue whether the grievor disobeyed an order or whether the order was illegal? Thinking through the issues can be the single most important factor to the success of your case. After all, whether your conclusions are correct depends upon how the questions are defined.

Reviewing the Evidence

In dealing with the evidence, do not simply regurgitate the testimony of witnesses in the sequence in which it was given. Instead, relate the testimony to the issues before the arbitrator, emphasize the evidence which supports your case, and attack the evidence which does not. You may, for example, bring together the testimony of witnesses dealing with a particular point, and comment on the quality of their evidence. Where there is a conflict among witnesses, you should give reasons why the evidence of your witnesses should be preferred. Your notes should set out the evidence relating to the points you wish to establish, the witnesses' testimony, and the relevant documents which have been filed as exhibits. It may be helpful for this purpose, if the documents are numerous and time permits, to prepare a binder of exhibits, and to provide the arbitrator with a copy.

While it is rare that you will be able to show that a witness is deliberately lying, you will more often be able to question a witness' motives, or cast doubt on the witness' recollection of events, or opportunity to observe them. Not only may you point to contradictions between the evidence of your witness and that of your adversary's witnesses, but you should, if possible, point out any conflict among your opponent's witnesses, and any inconsistency between the evidence given by your opponent's witnesses in chief and on cross-examination. Do not omit reference to any confirmatory evidence that bolsters your case.

In the event of a conflict among witnesses, the arbitrator may have to determine credibility. In this regard, the four main criteria are the witness' demeanour, opportunity to observe, interest or bias, and the inherent probabilities of the testimony. In this regard, it is worthwhile to set out the comments of Justice O'Halloran of the British Columbia Court of Appeal in *Faryna v. Chorny*:[27]

> "If a trial judge's finding of credibility is to depend solely on which person he thinks made the better appearance of sincerity in the witness box, we are left with a purely arbitrary finding and justice would then depend upon the best actors in the witness box. On reflection it becomes almost axiomatic that the appearance of telling the truth is but one of the elements that enter into the credibility of the evidence of a witness. Opportunities for knowledge, powers of observation, judgment and memory, ability to describe clearly what he has seen and heard, as well as other factors, combine to produce what is called credibility, and cf. *Raymond v. Bosanquet* (1919), 50 D.L.R. 560 at p.566, 59 S.C.R. 452 at p.460, 17 O.W.N. 295. A witness by his manner may create a very unfavourable impression of his truthfulness upon the trial Judge, and yet the surrounding circumstances in the case may point decisively to the conclusion that he is actually telling the truth. I am not referring to the comparatively infrequent cases in which a witness is caught in a clumsy lie.
>
> The credibility of interested witnesses, particularly in cases of conflict of evidence, cannot be gauged solely by the test of whether the personal demeanour of the particular witness carried conviction of the truth. The test must reasonably subject his story to an examination of its consistency with the probabilities that surround the currently existing conditions. In short, the real test of the truth of the story of a witness in such a case must be its harmony with the preponderance of the probabilities which a practical and informed person would readily recognize as reasonable in that place and in those conditions. Only thus can a Court satisfactorily appraise the testimony of quick-minded, experienced and confident witnesses, and those shrewd persons adept in the half-lie and of long and successful experience in combining skilful exaggeration with partial suppression of the truth. Again a witness may testify what he sincerely believes to be true, but he may be quite honestly mistaken. For a trial Judge to say 'I believe him because I judge him to be telling the truth', is to come to a conclusion on consideration of only half the problem. In truth it may easily be self-direction of a dangerous kind.

27 [1952] 2 D.L.R. 354, at pp.356-7.

> The trial Judge ought to go further and say that evidence of the witness he believes is in accordance with the preponderance of probabilities in the case and, if his view is to command confidence, also state his reasons for that conclusion. The law does not clothe the trial Judge with a divine insight into the hearts and minds of the witnesses. And a Court of Appeal must be satisfied that the trial Judge's finding of credibility is based not on one element only to the exclusion of others, but is based on all the elements by which it can be tested in the particular case."

In commenting on the consistency of the evidence with probabilities, you should consider whether the evidence of the opposite party's witnesses is consistent with human nature, known behaviour, or factual circumstances. A particular piece of circumstantial evidence may corroborate the testimony of your witnesses. But motive and demeanour are also important. You may be able to establish a motive that would discredit a witness' testimony, for example, that he or she wishes to bail a friend out of trouble. And, in the proper circumstances, you can comment directly upon the demeanour of witnesses. Were they evasive? Were they hesitant? Were they argumentative? All these approaches are useful, although the most important test in evaluating evidence is its consistency with probabilities. Your personal belief in the credibility of the grievor or other witnesses is, however, irrelevant.

You must not misstate the evidence, nor should you refer to facts that are not before the arbitrator, unless they are matters of common sense or general knowledge. On the other hand, you are free to suggest inferences or conclusions that should be drawn from the evidence. If a crucial witness is not called by your opponent, you can submit that an adverse inference should be drawn that his or her evidence would be unfavourable to your opponent's case. If your adversary fails to cross-examine one of your own witnesses on a particular point, you can similarly argue that the evidence of your witness should be accepted.

In an arbitration case, the party presenting the grievance must establish the facts on a balance of probabilities, although in a case where serious misconduct, such as criminal or quasi-criminal behaviour, is alleged, a higher degree of probability must be established, through the presentation of clear and cogent evidence. This is the standard of proof required at arbitration. Where the evidence is equally balanced, or clear and cogent evidence is lacking in a case involving criminal or quasi-criminal conduct, the party bearing the burden of proof will fail. In an appropriate case, you may want to argue that the opposite party bears the burden of proof, and has not satisfied it. On the other hand, the standard of proof comes into play only when the arbitrator cannot make up his or her mind about the facts. This does not happen that often.

Analyzing The Collective Agreement

In referring to the applicable provisions of the collective agreement, make sure you have a clear understanding as to how they fit together. Decide whether it is in your interest to urge that the contract be interpreted strictly or that it be construed liberally with a view to achieving the purpose of the parties. Remember that you cannot refer to "extrinsic evidence", such as past practice or negotiating history, unless the agreement is ambiguous, or there was a representation that the strict terms of the agreement would not be insisted upon (see estoppel).

If a plain reading of the agreement favours your interpretation, but past practice and negotiating history do not, you will likely want to argue that the agreement is clear and should be given its plain meaning. If the agreement is not crystal clear, but a liberal reading would be favourable to your interpretation, you may want to argue that the agreement should be read with a view to its purpose. If past practice or negotiating history support your position, you may want to argue that the agreement is ambiguous, so that extrinsic evidence can be considered in order to resolve its meaning. These arguments can be raised, in the alternative, though your argument will be more persuasive if it is consistent.

Some arbitrators consider that management has all the rights associated with control of the enterprise which are not expressly limited by the terms of the collective agreement. However, this so-called doctrine of reserved rights does not enjoy favour among most arbitrators, who regard a collective agreement as a bargain struck between equals. Indeed, there is a growing trend on the part of arbitrators, following a decision of the Ontario Court of Appeal,[28] to require that the parties carry out their obligations under the collective agreement in a manner that is fair, reasonable and in good faith. In presenting your argument as to the meaning of the contract, you should not ignore the doctrine of fairness.

28 *Municipality of Metropolitan Toronto v. C.U.P.E., Local 43* (1990), 69 D.L.R. (4th) 268 (Ont.C.A.).

Familiarize yourself with the principles of contract construction. Thus, it is important to examine a clause in the context of the whole agreement, including other provisions, so as to avoid inconsistencies. Headings, marginal notes, and the preamble itself, should be consulted in resolving questions of construction. Certain words or phrases may be imbued with particular meanings, as a result of rulings by arbitrators and courts. Thus, the word "shall" is ordinarily mandatory, i.e. it means that a party must do something, while "may" is ordinarily permissive, i.e. it means that a party has a discretion as to whether to do something or not. However, even here, the common usage of a term must yield to the language of the particular collective agreement.

Since it is presumed that all of the words in a contract were intended to have some meaning, every effort is made by arbitrators to reconcile the various provisions of the contract in order to give effect to its terms. In this connection, remember that a clause dealing with a matter in a specific way overrides a clause dealing with the same matter in more general terms. For example, where one clause provides generally for plant-wide seniority, but another provides for departmental seniority in a layoff, the latter clause will prevail in the event of a layoff.

Other canons of construction may also be applicable. Thus, according to the *"expressio unius"* rule, the express mention of one matter in the collective agreement implies the exclusion of related matters. For example, where a clause in a collective agreement specifies that a doctor's certificate must be obtained after three days absence due to illness, the *"expressio unius"* rule would result in a determination that the employer cannot automatically require a certificate before three days have elapsed. Some arbitrators have refused to apply the *"expressio unius"* rule on the ground that it is "a valuable servant, but a dangerous master", or that it is "continually relied on by despairing counsel, but very rarely applied by a court". However, despite repeated judicial cautions, arbitrators are occasionally persuaded by the *"expressio unius"* rule. Moreover, even where the maxim is not explicitly relied upon, the process of reasoning represented by it is often employed. If it helps your case, you should invoke it; if it does not, you should warn the arbitrator that it is dangerous to rely upon it.

The same is true of the so-called *"ejusdem generis"* rule. According to this rule, where particular items having a common characteristic are followed by general words, the items encompassed by these general words are to be limited to terms of the same type as those previously specified. Thus, where a clause requires the employer to supply shoes, jackets and trousers, and "anything else needed by the employees", the concluding words may be interpreted by an arbitrator, in light of the *"ejusdem generis"* rule, as being limited to items of clothing. Again, if the application of the rule supports your case, you should refer to it; if it does not, you can argue that the courts have warned against extending the *"ejusdem generis"* rule too far, and have said that care must always be taken that the application of the rule does not defeat the true intention of the parties.

The burden of proof does not apply to the determination of questions of law, including the interpretation of collective agreements. Here, regardless of the state of uncertainty that may be created by the parties' arguments, the arbitrator must make a determination as best as he or she can.

Presenting Legal Argument

Before you engage in a detailed review of the evidence, it is advisable to set out, in general terms, the principles of arbitration law which you intend to urge, and your theory of the case in relation to the factual conclusions which you propose to advance. A brief outline of this kind will enable the arbitrator to follow more easily your dissection of the evidence, and your analysis of the authorities, including text and awards. In short, set out the legal propositions in a simple fashion, and leave detailed reference for a later point in your argument. Thus, you may state: "The arbitration law, I submit, is to the effect that an order does not have to be obeyed if it requires the grievor to engage in an illegality" or, in another case, you might say: "Arbitrators are consistent in holding that an employee should not be discharged for innocent absenteeism".

While reference to the authorities is no doubt important, since arbitrators want to know what their peers have done when faced with similar problems, of much greater importance is the soundness of the rationale which you advance. Remember that arbitrators want, most of all, to decide what is the right thing to do in the circumstances of the case before them. In this regard, reasons are more persuasive than references. Thus, for example, do not content yourself with a reference to the numerous awards which rule that an employee should be paid for a statutory holiday which falls on what is for him or her a non-working day. Make it clear that the *rationale* for these rulings is that statutory holiday pay is part of the total monetary package, along with wages and other fringe benefits. At this stage of argument, you must persuade the arbitrator of the validity of the rationale behind the rule which you invoke.

You should consider whether or not you wish to advance alternative arguments, e.g. that the grievor did not assault the supervisor, but that, if he or she did, it was only because he or she was provoked. You may argue different conclusions as to the facts, and may advance alternative positions regarding the law. It is for the arbitrator to make the ultimate determination. It cannot be denied, however, that your case may be to some extent weakened if you take inconsistent alternative positions.

While it is useful to ponder in advance the arguments which the opposing advocate may raise, be careful about anticipating them, i.e. raising them before your adversary does. If you do argue in anticipation, you may simply succeed in raising matters that your counterpart may not have thought of. On the other hand, try to present an argument which is proof against the points you anticipate will be raised against it, and do not avoid dealing with those points, if your opponent should make them.

Citing Relevant Authorities

When referring to authorities, begin with relevant passages from the leading texts on arbitration, i.e. Brown and Beatty on *Canadian Labour Arbitration* and Palmer on *Collective Agreement Arbitration in Canada*. Then refer to the relevant excerpts from the most recent leading case in your favour, as reported in the series *Labour Arbitration Cases*. References to other texts, dictionaries and commentaries may be useful. Applicable legislation should also be cited.

In referring to authorities, do not omit details regarding their citation, e.g. in the case of a text, the title, the name of the author, the year of publication, the page reference; in the case of an award, the names of the parties, the identity of the arbitrator, the date of the award, the volume number of the report, the page number where the case begins and the page number where the relevant passage may be found. When citing the report series, *Labour Arbitration Cases*, indicate whether you are referring to the first series of volumes, or the second, third or fourth. If it is not too long, quote the relevant passage from the award, but remember that arbitrators can read, and that you should avoid a wearisome recitation of material that is extensive. There is no need to swamp the arbitrator with authorities. The leading cases, the relevant passages from the major texts, and short quotations should be sufficient.

You should be in a position to set out the facts of cases which support your position, as well as the principles for which they stand, and you should be prepared in advance to distinguish the cases which are likely to be cited by your opponent. You may seek to distinguish unfavourable cases on the ground that the facts in your case are different, or that the issue is not identical, or that the clauses in your collective agreement produce a contrary result, but if unfavourable decisions cannot be distinguished, you should explain why the reasoning in those cases which support your position is to be preferred.

Remember that it is not the quantity of the awards that will persuade the arbitrator, but their quality. Some awards—so-called leading cases—are more persuasive than others, because they have been adopted by numerous arbitrators. Moreover, the influence of an award may be enhanced by the reputation of the arbitrator who decided it. Awards of major arbitrators obviously command considerable influence, especially if they contain a careful analysis of the law. Be especially alert to previous awards of the arbitrator before whom you are appearing, since these may give you a hint of his or her approach to the issues. Look for relevant earlier awards between the same parties.

When you are referring to a text or an award, you should under no circumstances make misleading statements about the law. Be fair in your reading of the passages that you quote. If you are selective, your opponent will point this out, and this will undermine the arbitrator's confidence in your advocacy, not only in the particular case, but in any future case in which you appear before him or her. You are of course entitled to emphasize the merits of your own position, and to put it in as favourable a light as you can, but you must be accurate regarding your references to the law. To enable the arbitrator to follow your argument, it is advisable to make copies for the arbitrator of decisions or passages of texts which you intend to cite, and it is a matter of courtesy to provide copies to your opponent. Preparation of a casebook or book of authorities, or even a memorandum listing decisions, can also be helpful, and a copy should be provided to the arbitrator.

A caution. Most grievance arbitration cases turn on findings of fact. This is especially true for discharge and discipline cases; indeed, in these cases, once the facts are established, the outcome hinges largely on the exercise of the arbitrator's discretion, based on facts that vary with each case. In neither of these areas—fact-finding and the exercise of discretion—is legal research particularly profitable. The scope of legal research is more extensive in cases involving contract interpretation, but again here much turns on the wording of particular provisions of the collective agreement. Even where legal principles are relevant, citation of awards is secondary in importance to persuading the arbitrator of the equities of your case, and the soundness of your submission.

Requesting The Remedy

In requesting a remedy, you should be precise: you may request a declaration that the contract has been violated, a direction to comply with the contract, compensation for wages and other lost benefits. Make sure that you do not omit any possible remedy. In a proper case, you may want to ask the arbitrator to retain jurisdiction, in the event the grievance is upheld, for the purpose of determining remedies, such as compensation in the case of discharge without just cause.

Arguing In Rebuttal

The rebuttal should follow the same form as the argument in chief, save of course that it presents the other side of the case. Remember that rebuttal will be your only opportunity to make your case and respond to your opponent's submissions. So use the opportunity in full.

You may wish to deliver your own argument and then rebut directly the points made by your opponent in his or her argument in chief. Or you may do the reverse. Or you may integrate your own argument with a rebuttal of your adversary's case. This is a matter of individual style, and may vary from case to case. With this in mind, if you are presenting argument in rebuttal, you should make notes of the principal points made by your opponent, and flag those points in particular which you intend to address in rebuttal.

In no case should you misstate your opponent's position, or ignore it, or treat it with disdain. Attempt to state your opponent's argument fairly, and then provide a clear, cogent and concise answer to it. If your opponent's argument is not relevant, say so and explain why.

Delivering Reply Argument

The purpose of reply argument is to afford an opportunity to respond to new arguments or submissions that have been advanced in rebuttal. If you are delivering a reply, you may not use it as another opportunity to repeat and expand upon points that you have already made in your argument in chief. On the other hand, the right of reply can be used very effectively to narrow the crucial issues in dispute, while driving home your position. It is not always easy to draw a line, and arbitrators differ in the latitude they will allow. Much will depend upon the vigilance of the advocate in objecting to improper reply.

Sources of Arbitration Law

Sources of arbitration law, together with methods of abbreviation and citation, are set out at the end of this chapter. Sources include texts, digests, newsletters, case reports, journals and yearbooks. A text is a synopsis of the principles of arbitration law with footnotes citing the cases or awards which support the propositions contained in the text. Digests are summaries of cases and clauses relating to collective agreement arbitration. Newsletters are monthly or regular services containing a review and analysis of current legal developments in labour and employment law. A case report is a publication containing the entire text of grievance arbitration awards as they appear. Journals and yearbooks are periodic or annual volumes containing articles and studies on labour and employment law.

SOURCES OF ARBITRATION LAW

TEXTS

Brown and Beatty, *Canadian Labour Arbitration*
(Canada Law Book, 1990)
This text, published in loose-leaf format, is written by a lawyer and a law professor, and is arranged according to subject matter, e.g. seniority, discipline. The chapters are divided into subsections which are given a "key number". This key number is correlated with the report series, *Labour Arbitration Cases*. An extensive table of contents and index are included. Do not hesitate to quote portions of the book to an arbitrator if they support your case.

Palmer, *Collective Agreement Arbitration in Canada*
(Butterworths, 1990)
The author is a law professor. This text is also arranged according to subject matter. It is particularly useful because it contains many quotations from arbitration awards. A comprehensive table of contents and index are included. Again, it is useful to quote portions of the book, if they are helpful to your case, to the arbitrator.

Sack and Poskanzer, *Contract Clauses, Second Edition*
(Lancaster House, 1985)
The authors are labour lawyers. This is a 475-page text on collective agreement language in Canada, with 600 clauses from collective agreements in all sectors across Canada, and a clause-by-clause review of applicable legislation and arbitration law. A Clausefinder enables the reader to quickly locate any one of the hundreds of clauses in the text. The book also sets out principles of construction which arbitrators apply in interpreting collective agreement language.

DIGESTS

Canadian Labour Arbitration Summaries **(C.L.A.S.)**
This service, published by Canada Law Book, contains weekly summaries of most arbitration awards issued across Canada. This series is cross-referenced to the text by Brown and Beatty on *Canadian Labour Arbitration*. A cumulative subject index, together with a table of cases, is issued quarterly, and a volume listing all awards summarized since the inception of the series was published in 1992.

Krashinsky and Sack, *Discharge and Discipline* **(Lancaster House, 1989)**
The authors are labour lawyers. This text contains summaries of 500 discipline and discharge cases that have gone to arbitration over a 10-year period from 1978 to 1987. The cases are arranged according to the nature of the offence. Cases dealing with over 50 offences are included, relating to the following types of misconduct: attendance at work, insubordination, conflict of interest, disloyalty, theft, vandalism, dishonesty, work performance problems, abuse of fellow employees and others, alcohol and drug offences, union activity, and off-duty conduct. The book also contains a summary of the basic rules relating to discharge and discipline.

NEWSLETTERS

Lancaster Labour Law Reports (Lancaster House)

This publication is a newsletter which summarizes, quotes and evaluates significant decisions of arbitrators, tribunals and courts dealing with labour and employment law. The Reports include sections entitled *Labour Arbitration News, Labour Law News, Contract Clauses, Pension and Benefit Law Bulletin, Health and Safety Law, Charter Cases / Human Rights Reporter,* as well as a *Legislative Update.* Additional newsletters cover specific areas, and are entitled: *Construction Industry Employment Law, Education Employment Law, Employment Equity Reporter, Firefighters Employment Law, Health Care Employment Law, International Labour and Employment Law, Municipal Employment Law, Police Employment Law, Public Service and Crown Agency Employment Law, Women's / Pay Equity Employment Law,* and *Wrongful Dismissal Employment Law.*

CASE REPORTS

Labour Arbitration Cases (L.A.C.)

This report series, published by Canada Law Book, is presently in its fourth series. Several volumes appear per year. It contains awards from across Canada on all arbitration topics. The volumes are indexed, and a cumulative index is published periodically. Each award is reproduced verbatim and is prefaced by a listing of the issues involved in the award. The report of each case refers to the "key number" used in Brown and Beatty's text on *Canadian Labour Arbitration,* thus making it easy to check that text for the general principles and arbitral jurisprudence dealing with the same subject.

Awards in the first series are mainly, though not only, written by County Court judges who acted as arbitrators during the period in question. The cases contained in subsequent series—referred to more frequently since they are more recent—are mainly the product of law professors and professional arbitrators. The *Labour Arbitration Cases* series is abbreviated as L.A.C. Cases are referred to by giving the following information: names of company and union; volume number; report series; page number; name of arbitrator; and date of award, e.g. *C.U.P.E. Local 43 and Metro Toronto,* 21 L.A.C. (2d) 424 (Brent).

Other special report series

Some unions, such as the C.A.W., U.S.W.A., and C.U.P.E., print reports of their own awards. Some tribunals, such as the federal Public Service Staff Relations Board and the Ontario Grievance Settlement Board, will make available copies of their decisions. Some governments, such as that in Newfoundland, publish reports of cases decided in their jurisdictions. Make sure that you obtain awards which apply particularly to your jurisdiction, and your sector.

TEXTS ON EVIDENCE

Sopinka, Lederman and Bryant, *The Law of Evidence in Canada* **(Butterworths, 1992).**

This is the leading text on the law of evidence in Canada. Written by a judge of the Supreme Court of Canada, a practising lawyer and a law professor, it is 1,068-pages in length, and explores virtually every area of the law of evidence in exhaustive detail. However, it does not deal with labour arbitration.

Gorsky, Usprich and Brandt, *Evidence and Procedure in Canadian Labour Arbitration* **(Carswell, 1991).**

This is a loose-leaf volume, authored by several arbitrators and law professors. As the title suggests, it deals with the law of evidence and procedure in Canadian labour arbitration. It is updated on a periodic basis.

JOURNALS AND YEARBOOKS

Canadian Labour Law Journal **(C.L.L.J.)**

This journal, published on a quarterly basis by Butterworths and Lancaster House since 1991, contains articles by practitioners, arbitrators and academics dealing with labour and employment law. Approximately eight articles appear in each quarterly issue, together with reviews of books dealing with labour relations.

Labour Arbitration Yearbook **(Lab.Arb.Yb.)**

This series, also inaugurated in 1991 by Butterworths and Lancaster House, consists of annual volumes of articles devoted exclusively to grievance and interest arbitration. The articles are written by academics, arbitrators and lawyers, and they deal with topics of current concern, as well as matters relating to process and procedure. Approximately 20 articles are contained in each volume. These Yearbooks are the major source of legal research regarding issues arising in Canadian labour arbitration.

Abbreviations and Citations

STATUTES

S.C.	Statutes of Canada
R.S.C.	Revised Statutes of Canada
S.A.	Statutes of Alberta
R.S.A.	Revised Statutes of Alberta
S.B.C.	Statutes of British Columbia
R.S.B.C.	Revised Statutes of British Columbia
S.M.	Statutes of Manitoba
R.S.M.	Revised Statutes of Manitoba
S.N.B.	Statutes of New Brunswick
R.S.N.B.	Revised Statutes of New Brunswick
S.Nfld.	Statutes of Newfoundland
R.S.Nfld.	Revised Statutes of Newfoundland
S.N.S.	Statutes of Nova Scotia
R.S.N.S.	Revised Statutes of Nova Scotia
S.O.	Statutes of Ontario
R.S.O.	Revised Statutes of Ontario
S.P.E.I.	Statutes of Prince Edward Island
R.S.P.E.I.	Revised Statutes of Prince Edward Island
S.Q.	Statutes of Quebec
R.S.Q.	Revised Statutes of Quebec
S.S.	Statutes of Saskatchewan
R.S.S.	Revised Statutes of Saskatchewan

LABOUR TRIBUNALS AND COURTS

B.C.L.R.B.	British Columbia Labour Relations Board
C.A.	Court of Appeal
C.H.R.C.	Canadian Human Rights Commission
C.L.R.B.	Canada Labour Relations Board
Dist. Ct.	District Court
Div. Ct.	Divisional Court
Fed. C.A.	Federal Court of Appeal
F.C.T.D.	Federal Court, Trial Division
O.C.J.	Ontario Court of Justice
(J.C.)P.C.	Judicial Committee of Privy Council
O.L.R.B.	Ontario Labour Relations Board
Prov. Ct.	Provincial Court
P.S.S.R.B.	Public Service Staff Relations Board
Q.B.	Queen's Bench
Q.L.C.	Quebec Labour Court
Q.S.C.	Quebec Superior Court
S.C.	Supreme Court
S.C., App. Div.	Supreme Court, Appellate Division
S.C.C.	Supreme Court of Canada
W.C.B.	Workers' Compensation Board

CANADIAN LAW REPORTS

Admin. L.R.	Administrative Law Reports
A.P.R.	Atlantic Provinces Reports
Can. L.R.B.R.	Canadian Labour Relations Boards Reports
C.H.R.R.	Canadian Human Rights Reporter
C.L.L.C.	Canadian Labour Law Cases
C.R.R.	Canadian Rights Reports
di	decisions/information (Canada Labour Relations Board)
D.L.R.	Dominion Law Reports
Emp. L.R.	Employment Law Reports
L.A.C.	Labour Arbitration Cases
N.R.	National Reporter
O.A.C.	Ontario Appeal Cases
OLRB Rep.	Ontario Labour Relations Board Reports
O.R.	Ontario Reports
S.C.R.	Supreme Court Reports
W.W.R.	Western Weekly Reports

LANCASTER LABOUR LAW REPORTS

P.B.L.B.	Pension and Benefit Law Bulletin
C.C.	Contract Clauses
C.C./H.R.R.	Charter Cases/Human Rights Reporter
H. & S.L.	Health & Safety/Workers' Compensation Law
L.A.N.	Labour Arbitration News
L.L.N.	Labour Law News
L.U.	Legislative Update

Illustration of Case Citation

Toronto Star (1984), 11 L.A.C. (3d) 49 (Swan)

CASE NAME	YEAR OF REPORT	VOLUME NUMBER	TITLE OF REPORT (LABOUR ARBITRATION CASES)	THIRD SERIES	PAGE NUMBER	NAME OF ARBITRATOR

Footnotes and Headnotes

affd.	affirmed
apld.	applied
aprvd.	approved
cf.	compare
consd.	considered
contra	opposed
disaprvd.	disapproved
distd.	distinguished
et seq.	and following
expld.	explained
ff.	following pages
fn.	footnote
folld.	followed
ibid. (ibidem)	in the book or other publication cited directly above
id. (idem)	used where *ibid.* is qualified, e.g. *id.*, at p.46
infra	below
loc. cit. (loco citato)	in the same book or other publication cited previously, but not directly above
n.	note
op. cit. (opere citato)	used where *loc. cit.* is qualified, e.g. *op.cit.*, at p.72
passim	in various places throughout
pp.	pages
refd. to	referred to
revd.	reversed
sed	but
supra	above; used in referring to cases cited earlier
vide	see
videlicet (viz.)	to wit, namely

III
AFTER
THE
HEARING

CHAPTER 13

Issuing
the Award

Deliberations

Arbitrators usually deliver their awards in writing, some time after
the hearing. In Ontario, arbitrators are now empowered by statute
to give oral reasons promptly after the hearing, although either party
can request written reasons. The process of decision-making will
vary, of course, where a three-person arbitration board is involved.
In these circumstances, before rendering a decision, the chair will
consult with the parties' nominees, ordinarily in an executive session
and through the circulation of a draft award. When the final award
is issued, the parties' nominees are given an opportunity to concur
or dissent.

Sources

In reaching a decision, an arbitrator may refer to a number of sources,
including the evidence, the collective agreement, arbitration awards
and court decisions, dictionaries, statutes, and, in certain cases,
previous agreements, negotiating history, and past practice. Unlike
the courts, arbitrators are not bound by a doctrine of precedent. Thus,
while the decisions of other arbitrators may have persuasive value,
they are not automatically followed. However, where a case involves
a dispute between the same parties, regarding the same issues, an
arbitrator is not likely to depart from a previous award on the matter
unless it is considered to be plainly wrong.

Remedies

Insofar as remedies are concerned, arbitrators have a power, inherent in the adjudicative process, to grant appropriate remedies: they
can imply terms, and award such remedies as reinstatement, compensation, directions to comply, etc. However, while the principle of
estoppel is applicable to collective agreements, the doctrine of frus-

tration is not; as a result, it is not open to a party to repudiate the agreement in mid-term because of non-compliance by the other party. Moreover, arbitrators have no inherent power to amend or modify the collective agreement, unless it conflicts with statute, and arbitrators are divided as to their power to rectify the collective agreement, i.e. correct the language of the contract, even where it does not express the true intention of the parties. On the other hand, arbitrators have been given statutory power to modify a discharge or disciplinary penalty.

Time Limits

In some jurisdictions, time limits are set out in labour relations legislation for the issuance of awards. Thus, in Ontario, the *Labour Relations Act* now requires that a single arbitrator issue a decision within 30 days after the hearing (60 days in the case of an arbitration board), unless the parties consent to an extension or reasons are given for exceeding the time limit.

Reserving Jurisdiction

In some cases, arbitration boards will retain jurisdiction (remain "seized" of the matter), in the event the grievance is upheld, to adjudicate the issue of remedies, if the parties are not able to agree. Frequently, in discharge cases, the arbitration board will reserve jurisdiction to determine the amount of lost wages if the parties cannot reach agreement on the issue.

Re-Opening the Hearing

Before the award is issued, arbitrators have a discretion as to whether to re-open a hearing for the purpose of entertaining fresh evidence or further arguments, but such a discretion is exercised sparingly, and generally only where the evidence could not have been obtained with reasonable diligence prior to the hearing, and it would have a material affect on the outcome of the case.

Amending the Award

Once an arbitration board has issued a final decision, it is considered to have exhausted its jurisdiction, and therefore to be *"functus officio"*, unless all the issues have not been addressed. However, while an arbitration board has no jurisdiction to alter the final award after it is issued, it may clarify or complete the award or correct a clerical error.

Costs

So far as the costs of arbitration proceedings are concerned, arbitrators have generally held that, in the absence of language to the contrary in the collective agreement, they do not have the power to impose costs upon either party. Indeed, most collective agreements provide that the costs of arbitration are to be shared in equal proportions by both parties. However, in some cases, where an adjournment is granted, an arbitrator will impose payment of costs as a term or condition of the adjournment.

CHAPTER 14

Enforcement and Judicial Review

Enforcing the Award

Canadian labour legislation generally provides a method of enforcement of arbitration awards where one party or the other refuses to comply. In Ontario, the award may be filed in the Ontario Court of Justice and enforced in the same way as a judgment of the court, i.e. by way of contempt proceedings, which may result in committal to jail or a fine for non-compliance.

Reviewing the Award

Strictly speaking, there is no appeal from the award of an arbitrator. However, the courts possess an inherent jurisdiction to supervise the functioning of statutory tribunals, and as a result arbitration awards can be challenged in the courts on limited grounds, as where:

    (1) the arbitrator is biased, or has denied a fair hearing;

    (2) the arbitrator has made a jurisdictional error, e.g. an error relating to a legislative provision limiting the arbitrator's remedial powers, a patently unreasonable interpretation of a collective agreement, etc.

Factual determinations made by an arbitrator will not be disturbed by the courts, unless there is no evidence whatsoever to support them, and a large measure of deference is paid to an arbitrator's interpretation of a collective agreement unless the interpretation is patently unreasonable. On the other hand, little deference is paid by the courts to an interpretation by an arbitrator of common law principles or of legislative provisions, especially where they fall outside the arbitrator's "core area of expertise". In such cases, the courts will quash the arbitrator's interpretation if it is not correct.

In British Columbia, an arbitration award may be reviewed by the Labour Relations Board where a party has been or is likely to be denied a fair hearing, or where the award is inconsistent with the principles expressed or implied in the province's labour relations legislation. However, British Columbia remains an exception in this regard.

The principles of judicial review have recently been canvassed by the Supreme Court of Canada. In determining whether a matter falls within the jurisdiction of an arbitrator, the Supreme Court has adopted a "functional and pragmatic analysis". As it has in the past, the court will take into account the effect of a privative clause purporting to restrict the court's jurisdiction to review, and in doing so will be influenced by the strength of language used by the legislature. However, besides the wording of the legislative provision conferring jurisdiction (including the existence and nature of a privative clause), the Court will also consider the reason for the tribunal's existence, the area of expertise of the tribunal and the nature of the problem before the tribunal.

If the application of this analysis results in a finding that the issue is one confided to the jurisdiction of the tribunal to decide, the court will defer to the tribunal, unless the tribunal's decision is patently unreasonable. If it results in a finding that the issue is not confided to the tribunal's jurisdiction, the Court will intervene if the tribunal's decision is not correct.

Thus, in *Dayco*, the Supreme Court held that an arbitrator's decision as to whether a collective agreement was in existence did not relate to a matter confided to his jurisdiction; thus, it was subject to judicial review for correctness. The Court, however, indicated that, if the question had simply involved the interpretation of a collective agreement, the arbitrator's decision would not be interfered with unless it were patently unreasonable. In *Bradco*, the Supreme Court held that a decision by an arbitrator as to whether ambiguity existed in a collective agreement, so as to permit consideration of extrinsic evidence (a conciliator's report), was within the jurisdiction of the arbitrator. In these circumstances, the Court ruled that the arbitrator's decision should not be disturbed unless it was patently unreasonable.[29]

29 *See Dayco (Canada) Ltd. v C.A.W.-Canada* (1993), 102 D.L.R. (4th) 609 (S.C.C.), referring to *Syndicat national des employés de la Commission scolaire régionale de l'Outaouais v. Bibault,* [1988] 2 S.C.R. 1048 (S.C.C.) See also: *United Brotherhood of Carpenters v. Bradco Construction Ltd.* (1993), 102 D.L.R. (4th) 402 (S.C.C.); *Syndicat des employés professionels v. Université du Québec à Trois-Rivières* (1993), 101 D.L.R. (4th) 494 (S.C.C.); *Attorney General of Canada v. Public Service Alliance of Canada* (1993), 101 D.L.R. 4th 673 (S.C.C.); *Domtar Inc. v. Québec,* [1993] 2 S.C.R. 756 (S.C.C.)

CONCLUSION

The Ethics of Advocacy

Lawyers are bound by rules of ethics which are enforced by provincial law societies. Each law society has issued its own standards, but those issued by the Law Society of Upper Canada are typical. Rule 10 includes provisions which require that lawyers fearlessly ask every question and advance every argument that will help the client's case, provided this can be done honourably, and the tribunal is treated candidly and respectfully. Lawyers are prohibited from knowingly misstating facts or law; knowingly asserting something for which there is no reasonable basis in evidence; and deliberately failing to inform the tribunal of any pertinent authority which the lawyer considers to be directly on point and which has not been mentioned by an opponent. Subject to this, the Rules recognize that "In adversary proceedings the lawyer's function as advocate is openly and necessarily partisan", and that therefore "the lawyer is not obliged ... to assist an adversary, or advance matters derogatory to the client's case". There is a duty, however, to be accurate, candid and comprehensive when opposing interests are not represented.

As is well known, many arbitration cases are presented by non-lawyers, union representatives or management personnel. Do the rules of advocacy apply to them? Obviously not in the sense that they apply to lawyers, who constitute a self-governing profession, with statutory powers to regulate and discipline. But a violation of these standards will no doubt be considered offensive by arbitrators where the fairness of the process is undermined. In large part, your effectiveness as an advocate will depend on your reputation for fairness and integrity. These are qualities that have intrinsic worth; given the limited number of arbitrators, they are also essential to your success.

It is noteworthy, in this regard, that the Ontario Labour-Management Arbitrators' Association has adopted a Code of Ethics which states: "In the absence of an agreement by all parties, an arbitrator must provide a fair and adequate hearing in all respects consistent with the principles of natural justice and consistent with all applicable rules and procedures provided by law, which assures that all parties have sufficient opportunity to present their respective evidence and argument." Indeed, Ontario's labour legislation has been amended to authorize arbitrators to make such orders or give such directions as they consider appropriate "to expedite the proceedings or to prevent the abuse of the arbitration process".

Above all, it must be emphasized that the object of advocacy is to persuade. The person to be persuaded is the arbitrator. Since this is so, it makes no sense to be rude, provocative or antagonistic; to the contrary, it should be your aim to adopt a professional manner, both to the arbitrator and to the opposing advocate, while presenting your party's case in a cogent and convincing manner.

APPENDICES

Ontario Evidence Act, R.S.O. 1990, Chapter E.23

Requirement to Answer Questions

9. (1) A witness shall not be excused from answering any question upon the ground that the answer may tend to criminate the witness or may tend to establish his or her liability to a civil proceeding at the instance of the Crown or of any person or to a prosecution under any Act of the Legislature.

(2) If, with respect to a question, a witness objects to answer upon any of the grounds mentioned in subsection (1) and if, but for this section or any Act of the Parliament of Canada, he or she would therefore be excused from answering such question, then, although the witness is by reason of this section or by reason of any Act of the Parliament of Canada compelled to answer, the answer so given shall not be used or receivable in evidence against him or her in any civil proceeding or in any proceeding under any Act of the Legislature.

Cross-Examination as to Prior Inconsistent Statements

20. A witness may be cross-examined as to previous statements made by him or her in writing, or reduced into writing, relative to the matter in question, without the writing being shown to the witness, but, if it is intended to contradict the witness by the writing, his or her attention shall, before such contradictory proof is given, be called to those parts of the writing that are to be used for the purpose of so contradicting the witness, and the judge or other person presiding at any time during the trial or proceeding may require the production of the writing for his or her inspection, and may thereupon make such use of it for the purposes of the trial or proceeding as he or she thinks fit.

21. If a witness upon cross-examination as to a former statement made by him or her relative to the matter in question and inconsistent with his or her present testimony does not distinctly admit that he or she did make such statement, proof may be given that the witness did in fact make it, but before such proof is given the circumstances of the supposed statement sufficient to designate the particular occasion shall be mentioned to the witness, and the witness shall be asked whether or not he or she did make such statement.

23. A party producing a witness shall not be allowed to impeach his or her credit by general evidence of bad character, but the party may contradict the witness by other evidence, or, if the witness in the opinion of the judge or other person presiding proves adverse, such party may, by leave of the judge or other person presiding, prove that the witness made at some other time a statement inconsistent with his or her present testimony, but before such

last-mentioned proof is given the circumstances of the proposed statement sufficient to designate the particular occasion shall be mentioned to the witness and the witness shall be asked whether or not he or she did make such statement.

Cross-Examination as to Previous Convictions

22. (1) A witness may be asked whether he or she has been convicted of any crime, and upon being so asked, if the witness either denies the fact or refuses to answer, the conviction may be proved, and a certificate containing the substance and effect only, omitting the formal part, of the charge and of the conviction, purporting to be signed by the officer having the custody of the records of the court at which the offender was convicted, or by the deputy of the officer, is, upon proof of the identity of the witness as such convict, sufficient evidence of the conviction, without proof of the signature or of the official character of the person appearing to have signed the certificate.

(2) For such certificate, a fee of $1 and no more may be demanded or taken.

Admissibility of Business Records

35. (1) In this section,

"business" includes every kind of business, profession, occupation, calling, operation or activity, whether carried on for profit or otherwise; ("enterprise")

"record" includes any information that is recorded or stored by means of any device. ("document")

(2) Any writing or record made of any act, transaction, occurrence or event is admissible as evidence of such act, transaction, occurrence or event if made in the usual and ordinary course of any business and if it was in the usual and ordinary course of such business to make such writing or record at the time of such act, transaction, occurrence or event or within a reasonable time thereafter.

(3) Subsection (2) does not apply unless the party tendering the writing or record has given at least seven days' notice of the party's intention to all other parties in the action, and any party to the action is entitled to obtain from the person who has possession thereof production for inspection of the writing or record within five days after giving notice to produce the same.

(4) The circumstances of the making of such a writing or record, including lack of personal knowledge by the maker, may be shown to affect its weight, but such circumstances do not affect its admissibility.

(5) Nothing in this section affects the admissibility of any evidence that would be admissible apart from this section or makes admissible any writing or record that is privileged.

Admissibility of Medical Reports

52. (1) In this section,

"practitioner" means,

(a) a person licensed to practise under the *Health Disciplines Act*,

(b) a drugless practitioner registered under the *Drugless Practitioners Act*,

(c) a denture therapist under the *Denture Therapists Act*,

(d) a chiropodist registered under the *Chiropody Act*,

(e) a registered psychologist under the *Psychologists Registration Act*, or

(f) a person licensed or registered to practise in another part of Canada under an Act that is similar to an Act referred to in clause (a), (b), (c), (d) or (e).

(2) A report obtained by or prepared for a party to an action and signed by a practitioner and any other report of the practitioner that relates to the action are, with leave of the court and after at least ten days notice has been given to all other parties, admissible in evidence in the action.

(3)Unless otherwise ordered by the court, a party to an action is entitled, at the time that notice is given under subsection (2), to a copy of the report together with any other report of the practitioner that relates to the action.

(4)Except by leave of the judge presiding at the trial, a practitioner who signs a report with respect to a party shall not give evidence at the trial unless the report is given to all other parties in accordance with subsection (2).

(5)If a practitioner is required to give evidence in person in an action and the court is of the opinion that the evidence could have been produced as effectively by way of a report, the court may order the party that required the attendance of the practitioner to pay as costs therefor such sum as the court considers appropriate.

Rules of Civil Procedure (Ontario Courtof Justice) R.R.O. 1990, Reg. 194

Expert Witnesses

53.03 (1) A party who intends to call an expert witness at trial shall, not less than ten days before the commencement of the trial, serve on every other party to the action a report, signed by the expert, setting out his or her name, address and qualifications and the substance of his or her proposed testimony.

(2) No expert witness may testify, except with leave of the trial judge, unless subrule (1) has been complied with.

Re Winchester District Memorial Hospital and Ontario Nurses' Association

(1989), 8 L.A.C. (4th) 342 (Bendel)

Interim Award

The three grievances before the board relate to the same issue, namely, whether the grievors were entitled to be paid for time they spent taking certain courses outside of working hours. At the outset of the hearing, after the grievances and the collective agreement had been filed on consent, the parties advised the board that there was a procedural dispute between them which they wanted the board to decide as a preliminary matter. Since neither party was prepared to argue the matter that day, they agreed that the board should adjourn the hearing so as to allow them to make written submissions. Those written submissions have now been completed.

The procedural dispute between the parties has to do with a subpoena (or summons) *duces tecum* issued by the board at the request of the association, addressed to Ms. C. Manley, the assistant executive director of the hospital. The association's position, briefly stated, is that Ms. Manley is obliged, at the association's request, to hand over the documents listed in the subpoena without being sworn as a witness. The association's concern, it appears, is that if Ms. Manley becomes its witness, she would be subject to cross-examination by counsel for the hospital. The hospital's position is that the procedure sought by the association is tantamount to pre-hearing discovery, which, according to the case-law, is not available as a general proposition in grievance arbitrations under the *Labour Relations Act*, R.S.O. 1980, c.228, as amended, and that the proper procedure in response to a subpoena *duces tecum* is that the witness is asked to identify the documents listed in the subpoena after being sworn. The documents are only receivable in evidence, according to the hospital, if the party seeking to introduce them can satisfy the board as to their admissibility from the point of view of relevancy and cogency.

The prevalent view among arbitrators in Ontario (and in most other Canadian jurisdictions) is that, in the absence of some provision in the applicable collective agreement, they cannot order a party to produce documents in advance of the hearing. In *Re Fabricated Steel Products (Windsor) Ltd. and U.A.W., Loc. 195* (1977), 16 L.A.C. (2d) 148 (O'Shea), the arbitrator was asked to direct the employer, in advance of the hearing, to produce certain documents and to furnish certain particulars in relation to the discharge of the grievor. The arbitrator concluded that he was without power to issue the directions sought. At pp.160-1, the arbitrator said the following:

... apart from negotiated grievance procedures, there is nothing in s. 37 of the *Labour Relations Act* which authorizes an arbitrator to impose a pre-hearing or pre-trial procedure on the parties. An arbitrator must find his jurisdiction either under the provisions of the collective agreement or under the specific powers granted to him under the *Labour Relations Act*. An arbitrator has no "equitable jurisdiction" and I find no "inherent jurisdiction" in the *Labour Relations Act* to grant the remedy requested by the union. An arbitrator's jurisdiction is the creature of the collective agreement or the statute which may modify or enlarge the authority granted to him under the collective agreement.

Although an arbitrator may be said to have authority to establish his own procedures pursuant to the provisions of s. 37(7) of the Act, such procedures must be limited to procedures for the conduct of the hearing and relate to the acceptance of evidence. While some may argue that s. 37(7)(e) empowers an arbitrator to direct the production of documents at the request of one of the parties, I am unable to agree with that argument. Obviously, it would be contrary to the principles of natural justice for an arbitrator to authorize one of the parties to a dispute to act on the arbitrator's behalf for the purpose of exercising his authority under s. 37 of the *Labour Relations Act*.

What was referred to in *Re Fabricated Steel Products* as s.37(7) of the *Labour Relations Act* is now s.44(8) of the Act. It has not been amended since the *Fabricated Steel Products* award. It reads as follows:

44(8) An arbitrator or the chairman of an arbitration board, as the case may be, has power,

(a) to summon and enforce the attendance of witnesses and to compel them to give oral or written evidence on oath in the same manner as a court of record in civil cases; and

(b) to administer oaths,

and an arbitrator or an arbitration board, as the case may be, has power,

(c) to accept such oral or written evidence as the arbitrator or the arbitration board, as the case may be, in its discretion considers proper, whether admissible in a court of law or not;

(d) to enter any premises where work is being done or has been done by the employees or in which the employer carries on business or where anything is taking place concerning any of the differences submitted to him or it, and inspect and view any work, material, machinery, appliance or article therein, and interrogate any person respecting any such thing or any such differences;

(e) to authorize any person to do anything that the arbitrator or arbitration board may do under clause (d) and to report to the arbitrator or arbitration board thereon.

In R*e City of Peterborough and Peterborough Professional Fire Fighters Assn., Loc. 519* (1978), 19 L.A.C. (2d) 264 (H.D. Brown), the arbitrator sought to distinguish the award in *Re Fabricated Steel Products*. He suggested, at pp.270-1, that what had been at issue in the earlier case was an order for production in advance of the opening of the hearing, which was outside of the arbitrator's jurisdiction, whereas production could be ordered once the hearing had opened if the production was necessary to ensure a fair hearing:

> I am here not dealing with a pre-hearing procedure such as was dealt with in the *Re Fabricated Steel Products* case, *supra*, but where in that decision, there is any reference to the restriction of an arbitrator's authority to require the production of documents when he has taken jurisdiction at the hearing, I, with great respect, differ from such conclusions. The arbitrator does have the authority and responsibility to determine the procedure at the hearing and to afford the parties a fair hearing within the general principles of natural justice. Where it becomes obvious that [sic] the submissions of the parties, as in this case, that certain documents are necessary to be examined for the proper conduct of the grievance which must be determined by the arbitrator, it is inherently justified that the arbitrator follow generally the procedures available in Court proceedings, to require the relevant documents to be produced at the hearing or prior to a further hearing should that be necessary.

This attempt by the arbitrator in R*e City of Peterborough* to assert a basis upon which production of documents could be ordered has not met with acceptance in subsequent decisions: see *Re Falconbridge Nickel Mines Ltd.* and *Sudbury Mine, Mill & Smelter Workers Union, Loc. 598* (1981), 29 L.A.C. (2d) 224 (Kennedy), and *Re City of Guelph and Guelph Professional Firefighters Assn., Loc. 467* (1982), 5 L.A.C. (3d) 43 (Beatty).

It is obvious from this case-law that the issue being considered was whether arbitrators had the power under the applicable legislation to order the production of documents. The prevalent view is that no such power exists under the *Ontario Labour Relations Act*. Although there is a discussion in the cases on the desirability of pre-hearing procedures such as production of documents in arbitrations, that was not the main focus of the decisions. This case-law is therefore of little or no help, in our view, in trying to understand whether the production of documents can be obtained through some other means, specifically by the subpoena *duces tecum*, which is the process that the association in this case has chosen to use. The subpoena *duces tecum* is a distinct process. The procedure to be followed in relation to the subpoena *duces tecum* has to be determined according to the rules relating to such subpoenas. The rules relating to "production" are of little or no relevance. It is in the light of the case-law dealing with subpoenas that we will have to decide whether, as argued by the association, the obligation of a person served with a subpoena duces tecum is to transmit the documents sought to the party issuing the subpoena without first being sworn.

We would note that no question arises in this case as to our authority to issue a subpoena *duces tecum*. Any doubts on that score have been laid to rest by the decision in *Re Toronto Star and Southern Ontario Newspaper Guild* (1983), 11 L.A.C. (3d) 249 (Swan). The question we are called upon to decide relates to the procedure to be followed after the subpoena has been issued.

In *Heart Construction Co. Ltd.*, [1983] O.L.R.B. Rep. Jan. 84, the Ontario Labour Relations Board considered at length the right of the party at whose instance the subpoena *duces tecum* was issued to obtain the documents referred to in the subpoena. This is what the board said (at pp.85-7):

4. A *subpoena duces tecum* has been defined in Black's Law Dictionary as follows:

"A process by which the court, at the instances of a suitor, commands a witness who has in his possession or control some document or paper that is pertinent to the issues of a pending controversy, to produce it at trial."

There is no issue before the Board concerning its authority to issue a *subpoena duces tecum*. The nature and scope of the subpoena duces tecum is derived from a number of nineteenth century English cases. One of the earliest cases to deal with the point was Davis v. Dale (1830), 172 E.R. 729, where it became necessary to give in evidence certain written agreements. The agent who held them was served with a *subpoena duces tecum* and was subsequently called upon by the plaintiff to produce the documents without being sworn as a witness in the cause. The defendant argued that the course pursued by the party calling such a person assumed that he was in possession of the papers required, which assumption, it was claimed, the plaintiff had no right to make. The defendant also argued that the only way to ascertain this fact was for the question to be put to the agent, and the putting of the question would clearly render the agent as a witness, and entitle the other side to cross-examine. The court, through Lord Chief Justice Tindal, expressed the view that a person having custody of papers and being subpoenaed to produce them on the trial of a cause, may be called on to put them in without being sworn. Accordingly, the agent was not sworn and the defendant was not given an opportunity to cross-examine.

5. A few years later, support was expressed for the proposition that the *subpoena duces tecum* has two separate aspects in the comments of Parke, J., in *Perry v. Gibson* (1834), 110 E.R. 1125, 1126, where he stated:

"I always thought that a *subpoena duces tecum* had two distinct objects and that one might be enforced without the other."

Parke, J., made reference to the *ad testificandum* and the *duces tecum* aspects of the subpoena, with the first requiring attendance for the purpose of giving oral testimony and the latter requiring the person to attend and produce the documents which had been referred to. This point was further elucidated in the same year in *Summers v. Moseley* (1834), 149 E.R. 849, where Bayley, B., indicated that it does no follow that because a person is called upon to produce a document or documents that he must be called upon to give oral evidence. At page 853, he stated as follows:

> "The question which was very important as a rule of evidence, was, whether a bailiff having been called by the plaintiff to produce the warrant from the sheriff under which he had acted, had a right to insist upon being sworn in the ordinary form as a witness, so as to give the defendant an opportunity of cross-examining him, or whether the plaintiff in the cause had a right to insist upon the production of the warrant without the bailiff being sworn. Several cases were cited upon the argument as having been decided in conformity with the rule as contended for on behalf of the plaintiff, but they were all cases at Nisi Prius, and as the question is one of great importance and frequent occurrence, and it is highly desirable that the rule of evidence should be fixed, we were desirous of having an opportunity of communicating on the subject with the judges of the other courts before we delivered our judgment. We have accordingly had a communication with the other judges, and the result is, that we are of opinion that the cases ruled at Nisi Prius, and relied upon on behalf of the plaintiff, were rightly ruled, and that the officer is compellable to produce the document in his possession without being sworn, the party calling him to produce it not having occasion to ask him any question."

6. More recently in *Tribune Newspaper Company Limited v. Fort Frances Pulp and Paper Company Limited* (1932), 40 Man. R. 401, 409, Ronson, J.A., stated:

> "There is no need to elaborate the fact that a person subpoenaed in this way [subpoena duces tecum] may be called on to produce documents without being sworn, or he may be sworn and then submit to examination as to the existence, whereabouts or control of the documents."

Similarly, in *Cross on Evidence*, 4th Edition, the following comment appears:

> "Someone who simply produces a document pursuant to a *subpoena duces tecum* does not have to be sworn if there is another witness who can identify the document. This means that the person producing it cannot be cross-examined."

7. In Canadian texts, *Holmstead and Gale* states at page 1429 as follows:

> "The two phases of testimony, personal and documentary are required to be separate, and the summoning party is entitled to require the witness to produce the document without putting him on the stand to speak as to his general knowledge of the case."

The practice of having a document produced without swearing the witness is known as calling a witness on his subpoena and in *The Law of Evidence in Civil Cases* (1974), Sopinka and Lederman at page 499 refer to *Lyone v. Long*, [1917] 3 W.W.R. 139, which case sets forth a number of situations in which witnesses were not subject to cross-examination. One example of this exemption was:

> "A witness called merely to produce a document where the document requires no proof or is to be proved by other means."

The only authority brought to our attention that is at odds with the conclusion by the Ontario Labour Relations Board in *Heart Construction Ltd.*, *supra*, was the following dictum in *Re Fabricated Steel Products, supra* (followed in *Re Government of Alberta (Department of Advanced Education) and A.U.P.E.*, unreported decision of adjudicator Koshman of the Alberta Public Service Grievance Appeal Board, dated April 13, 1988), at pp.161-2:

> A party who wishes to have documents produced for the purpose of an arbitration hearing can request the arbitrator to issue a summons duces tecum to the person who has the custody or control of the documents and have that person in his testimony identify the documents at the hearing: see *Re Int'l Union of Operating Engineers, Local 955 and Henuset Bros. Ltd.* (1974), 49 D.L.R. (3d) 288, [1974] 6 W.W.R. 765.

We are satisfied, from our reading of the extensive case-law and the authoritative texts cited in *Heart Construction Ltd.*, that the party causing the subpoena duces tecum to be issued is entitled to have the documents which are listed in the subpoena handed over at the hearing without having to call the person served with the subpoena as its own witness. We should add that although the Ontario Labour Relations Board has broad powers to order the production of documents (pursuant to s. 103(2)(a) of the *Labour Relations Act*), we are satisfied that its statement of the law in *Heart Construction Ltd.* is just as applicable to a board of arbitration as it is to the Ontario Labour Relations Board itself. The lengthy passage cited from Heart Construction Ltd. is an examination of the law relating to subpoenas duces tecum, which that board, like a board of arbitration, is authorized to issue.

In our view, however, there is no authority for the production of the documents in advance of the hearing. The subpoena, on its face, requires the person served to attend at the hearing and bring documents to the hearing. It does not operate to require that documents be handed over in advance of the time and date set for the hearing.

That, however, is not the end of the matter. The hospital, in the present case, has questioned the relevance to the grievances before us of the documents that Ms. Manley has been asked to produce. It takes the view that the association has to lay a factual foundation in the evidence for the relevance of the documents it seeks. In addition to refusing to concede the relevance of the documentation in general, the hospital has raised a specific objection to the admissibility of some of the documents that Ms. Manley has been asked to produce, namely, that they were created before these parties had signed their first collective agreement.

It is obvious that the party seeking to have documents produced pursuant to a subpoena *duces tecum* cannot be allowed to go on a fishing expedition. It has to establish some rational link between the issues in dispute and the documents it seeks to obtain. In R*e City of Kanata and C.U.P.E., Loc. 2753* (1987), 29 L.A.C. (3d) 412 (Carrothers), the arbitrator concluded (at p.418) that the "appropriate test for determining what should be produced to the other side at the *duces tecum* stage is that of 'arguably relevant'". A party is only entitled to access to documents pursuant to a subpoena *duces tecum* if they are "arguably relevant" to the issues in dispute. The arbitrator continued as follows (at pp.420-1):

> On the matter of the test of "arguably relevant", I can speculate that counsel for the union will seek to use the report of the director of human resources to throw light on the substance of the change in job description and the state of the collective mind of city council. I can speculate further that counsel for the union wants the job descriptions in order to compare the job description of the deputy chief engineer with managerial positions and with bargaining unit positions. I can speculate also that the job descriptions of persons excluded from the bargaining unit because they are employed in a confidential capacity in respect of labour relations will be less useful to the exercise of comparison. But I should not act, positively or negatively, on any of those speculations unless or until they are converted into evidence, under oath or otherwise.
>
> . . . . .
>
> I therefore conclude that the arbitration hearing should reconvene and that counsel for the union should proceed to establish the factual base for the production of the documents in question as

counsel sees fit, and that I should make such orders or rulings as may be justified accordingly. If I were to order otherwise I would be cutting corners at the expense of the city's rights.

We accept that "arguable relevance" is the appropriate test for deciding whether particular documents listed in subpoena *duces tecum* have to be handed over in advance of the witness being sworn. However, we respectfully question the conclusion in *Re City of Kanata* to the effect that the only way arguable relevance can be established is through evidence already adduced. In the present case, the board has before it the collective agreement, the grievances and the "theory" of the association's case. Counsel for the association has explained to us, in his submissions, what he hopes to prove through each of the documents sought and how this is relevant to the case. We can see no good reason for not being satisfied that the arguable relevance of the documentation sought has been established through the material before us. We express no views, at this stage, as to whether any of the documents sought is sufficient relevant to be admissible. However, the materials referred to have persuaded us as to the arguable relevance of the documents.

The employer has argued that some of the documents sought cannot be relevant as they were created prior to the existence of a collective bargaining relationship. It is not immediately apparent to us why this should have any bearing on their relevance. But, in any event, we are not ruling definitively at this stage on the admissibility of the documents, merely on their arguable relevance. Even though the documents pre-dated the collective bargaining relationship between the parties, we accept their arguable relevance to the issues in dispute.

It is therefore our conclusion that Ms. Manley is obliged to provide the documents listed in the subpoena to the association when the hearing reconvenes. We should add, however, that it would obviously make good sense for these documents to be transmitted in advance of the hearing. The association will likely want some time to examine them before deciding whether they are indeed relevant to its case. Failing an opportunity for the association to examine them in advance of the hearing, an adjournment might be necessary, which would further delay the resolution of these grievances, filed in April, 1987. We echo the views of the arbitrator in *Re City of Kanata, supra,* at p.421:

> In my limited experience, when proceedings relating to a *subpoena duces tecum* reached the stage where this case now stands, counsel have divulged the documents to avoid an almost inevitable adjournment to give the party who obtained the subpoena an opportunity to study the documents and prepare his case accordingly. But this is a matter of volition, and it is not the role of the arbitrator to intervene.

The hearing will reconvene on a date to be communicated to the parties.

[B. Herlich concurring; W.K. Winkler, Q.C. dissenting]

Excerpt from *Re Greater Niagara Transit Commission and Amalgamated Transit Union, Local 1582*

(1987), 43 D.L.R. (4th) 71 (Ontario Divisional Court)

Justice Watt, for the Court, at pp. 88-90:

In addition to the general principles just described, it is also critical to bear in mind that an arbitration board is not strictly confined in its reception of evidence to admit only that which is receivable in a court of law.

Section 44(8)(c) of the *Labour Relations Act*, confers upon an arbitration board the power 'to accept such oral or written evidence as the...board...in its discretion considers proper, whether admissible in a court of law or not'. The clause, enacted in inclusionary terms, vests a wide range of discretion in the board in determining what evidence it shall receive. Relevance is not specifically mentioned in the clause as a rule or principle to be applied in determining the admissibility of evidence in arbitration proceedings, but it is difficult to envisage of what value oral or written evidence would be in such proceedings in the event that relevance were not applied as the main general rule underlying admissibility. It is easily the most important element in determining what is 'proper' to be received under s. 44(8)(c). Although the statutory discretion articulated in the clause is in inclusionary terms, that is to say it identifies in express terms that which may be received as evidence, *viz.* '...such oral or written evidence as the...board in its discretion, considers proper...', it necessarily implies or carries with it an exclusionary aspect in that what does not so qualify, by definition, is to be excluded from evidence in the proceedings. The clause also makes it clear that whether an item of evidence would be admissible if tendered in a court of law is not to affect a determination of whether it is receivable in proceedings before the board. To put the matter another way, there is no congruence, correspondence or equivalence between that which is receivable in a court of law and that which is admissible in arbitration proceedings. It follows, in my respectful view, from the plain wording of the clause, that an arbitration board is not to take as dispositive or determinative of an admissibility issue arising in arbitration proceedings a ruling of a court in allied or unrelated proceedings in which the selfsame evidence has been tendered for admission. Implicit in the enactment, in my respectful view, is a recognition that arbitration proceedings ought to be conducted less formally than legal proceedings, unencumbered by strict adherence to rules of evidence which may affect underlying policy considerations wholly inapplicable in the arbitration context.

It would appear clear that under s. 44(8)(c) an arbitration board, if it considered it proper so to do, could:

(i) receive evidence declared inadmissible;

(ii) exclude evidence declared admissible;

(iii) receive evidence declared admissible; or

(iv) exclude evidence declared inadmissible,

in legal proceedings before a court of competent jurisdiction. To put the matter in somewhat more general terms, the clause gives statutory effect to the apparent irrelevance of interlocutory evidentiary rulings made during the course of legal proceedings before a court of competent jurisdiction to a determination of admissibility in arbitration proceedings. Although it would not seem otherwise than a prudent or proper course for an arbitrator or board to receive relevant evidence which either has been or would be admissible if tendered in legal proceedings, it by no means follows that what has been there rejected, *ipso facto*, ought to be excluded in arbitration proceedings. Differences between the parties, the issues, the onus and quantum of necessary proof and, at all events, the absence in most instances of considerations of the nature that underlie the exclusionary canons of the law of evidence, most especially in criminal cases, together with the terms of the board's own evidentiary mandate, compel an independent assessment of the admissibility issue in arbitration proceedings.

Rules of Professional Conduct
Law Society of Upper Canada

The Lawyer as Advocate

RULE 10

When acting as an advocate the lawyer, while treating the tribunal with courtesy and respect, must represent the client resolutely and honourably within the limits of the law.

Commentary

Scope of the Rule

1. The principle of this Rule applies generally to the lawyer as advocate, and therefore extends not only to court proceedings but also to appearances and proceedings before boards, administrative tribunals and other bodies, regardless of their function or the informality of their procedures.

Abuse of Process

2. The lawyer has a duty to the client to raise fearlessly every issue, advance every argument, and ask every question, however distasteful, which the lawyer thinks will help the client's case and to endeavour to obtain for the client the benefit of every remedy and defence authorized by law. The lawyer must discharge this duty by fair and honourable means, without illegality and in an manner consistent with the lawyer's duty to treat the tribunal with candour, fairness, courtesy and respect.

The lawyer must not, for example:

(a) abuse the process of the tribunal by instituting or prosecuting proceedings which, although legal in themselves, are clearly motivated by malice on the part of the client and are brought solely for the purpose of injuring the other party;

(b) knowingly assist or permit the client to do anything which the lawyer considers to be dishonest or dishonourable;

(c) appear before a judicial officer when the lawyer, the lawyer's associates or the client have business or personal relationships with such officer which give rise to or might reasonably appear to give rise to pressure, influence or inducement affecting the impartiality of such officer;

(d) endeavour or allow anyone else to endeavour, directly or indirectly, to influence the decision or action of a tribunal or any of its officials in any case or matter by any means other than open persuasion as an advocate;

(e) knowingly attempt to deceive a tribunal or influence the course of justice by offering false evidence, misstating facts or law, presenting or relying upon a false or deceptive affidavit, suppressing what ought to be disclosed, or otherwise assisting in any fraud, crime or illegal conduct;

(f) knowingly misstate the contents of a document, the testimony of a witness, the substance of an argument or the provisions of a statute or like authority;

(g) knowingly assert something for which there is not reasonable basis in evidence, or the admissibility of which must first be established;

(h) deliberately refrain from informing the tribunal of any pertinent authority which the lawyer considers to be directly on point and which has not been mentioned by an opponent;

(i) dissuade a material witness from giving evidence, or advise such a witness to be absent;

(j) knowingly permit a witness to be presented in a false or misleading way, or to impersonate another;

(k) needlessly abuse, hector, or harass a witness;

(l) needlessly inconvenience a witness.

3. (a) The lawyer who has unknowingly done or failed to do something which if done or omitted knowingly would have been in breach of this Rule and who discovers it, has a duty to the court, subject to Rule 4 on Confidentiality of Information, to disclose the error or omission and do all that can reasonably be done in the circumstances to rectify it.

(b) If the client desires that a course be taken which would involve a breach of this Rule, the lawyer must refuse and do everything reasonably possible to prevent it. If that cannot be done the lawyer should, subject to Rule 8 on Withdrawal of Services, withdraw or seek leave to do so.

4. In civil proceedings, the lawyer has a duty not to mislead the court as to the position of the client in the adversary process. Thus, a lawyer representing a party to litigation who has made or is party to an agreement made before or during the trial whereby a plaintiff is guaranteed recovery by one or more parties notwithstanding the judgment of the court, shall forthwith reveal the existence and particulars of the agreement to the court and to all parties to the proceedings.

Unmeritorious Proceedings

5. The lawyer should never waive or abandon the client's legal rights, for example an available defence under a statute of limitations, without the client's informed consent. In civil matters it is desirable that the lawyer should avoid and discourage the client from resorting to frivolous or vexatious objections or attempts to gain advantage from slips or oversights not going to the real merits, or tactics which will merely delay or harass the

other side. Such practices can readily bring the administration of justice and the legal profession into disrepute.

Encouraging Settlements

6. Whenever the case can be fairly settled, the lawyer should advise and encourage the client to do so rather than commence or continue legal proceedings.

Courteousness

7. At all times the lawyer should be courteous and civil to the court and to those engaged on the other side. Legal contempt of court and the professional obligation outlined here are not identical, and a consistent pattern of rude, provocative or disruptive conduct by the lawyer, even though unpunished as contempt, might well merit discipline.

Undertakings

8. An undertaking given by the lawyer to the court or to another lawyer in the course of litigation must be strictly and scrupulously carried out. Unless clearly qualified, the lawyer's undertaking is a personal promise and responsibility.

Duty as Prosecutor

9. When engaged as a prosecutor, the lawyer's prime duty is not to seek to convict, but to see that justice is done through a fair trial upon the merits. The prosecutor exercises a public function involving much discretion and power, and must act fairly and dispassionately. The prosecutor should not do anything which might prevent the accused from being represented by counsel or communicating with counsel and, to the extent required by law and accepted practice, should make timely disclosure to the accused or defence counsel (or to the court if the accused is not represented) of all relevant and known facts and witnesses, whether tending to show guilt or innocence.

Duty as Defence Counsel

10. When defending an accused person, the lawyer's duty is to protect the client as far as possible from being convicted except by a tribunal of competent jurisdiction and upon legal evidence sufficient to support a conviction for the offence with which the client is charged. Accordingly, and not withstanding the lawyer's private opinion as to credibility or merits, the lawyer may properly rely upon any evidence or defences including so-called technicalities not known to be false or fraudulent.

11. Admissions made by the accused to the lawyer may impose strict limitations on the conduct of the defence, and the accused should be made aware of this. For example, if the accused clearly admits to the lawyer the factual and mental elements necessary to constitute the offence, the lawyer, if convinced that the admissions are true and voluntary, may properly take objection to the jurisdiction of the court, or to the form of the indictment, or to the admissibility or sufficiency of the evidence, but must not suggest

that some other person committed the offence, or call any evidence which, by reason of the admissions, the lawyer believes to be false. Nor may the lawyer set up an affirmative case inconsistent with such admissions, for example, by calling evidence in support of an alibi intended to show that the accused could not have done, or in fact had not done, the act. Such admissions will also impose a limit upon the extent to which the lawyer may attack the evidence for the prosecution. The lawyer is entitled to test the evidence given by each individual witness for the prosecution and argue that the evidence taken as a whole is insufficient to amount to proof that the accused is guilty of the offence charged, but the lawyer should go no further than that.

Agreement on Guilty Plea

12. Where, following investigation:

(a) the defence lawyer bona fide concludes and advises the accused client that an acquittal of the offence charged is uncertain or unlikely;

(b) the client is prepared to admit the necessary factual and mental elements;

(c) the lawyer fully advises the client of the implications and possible consequences, and particularly of the detachment of the court; and

(d) the client so instructs the lawyer,

it is not improper for the lawyer to have discussions with the prosecutor regarding a possible disposition of the case. The public interest must not, however, be sacrificed in pursuit of an apparently expedient means of disposing of doubtful cases.

Role in Adversary Proceedings

13. In adversary proceedings the lawyer's function as advocate is openly and necessarily partisan. Accordingly, the lawyer is not obliged (save as required by law or under subparagraph 2(h) and paragraph 9 above) to assist an adversary or advance matters derogatory to the client's case. When opposing interests are not represented, for example in ex parte or uncontested matters, or in other situations where the full proof and argument inherent in the adversary system cannot obtain, the lawyer must take particular care to be accurate, candid and comprehensive in presenting the client's case so as to ensure that the court is not misled.

Interviewing Witnesses

14. The lawyer may properly seek information from any potential witness (whether under subpoena or not) but should disclose the lawyer's interest and take care not to subvert or suppress any evidence or procure the witness to stay out of the way. An opposite party who is professionally represented should not be approached or dealt with save through or with the consent of that party's lawyer.

Communication with Witness giving Evidence

15. The lawyer should observe the following guidelines respecting communication with witnesses giving evidence:

(a) During examination-in-chief it is not improper for the examining lawyer to discuss with the witness any matter that has not been covered in the examination up to that point.

(b) During examination-in-chief by another lawyer of a witness who is unsympathetic to the lawyer's cause the lawyer not conducting the examination-in-chief may properly discuss the evidence with the witness.

(c) Between completion of examination-in-chief and commencement of cross-examination of the lawyer's own witness there ought to be no discussion of the evidence given in chief or relating to any matter introduced or touched upon during the examination-in-chief.

(d) During cross-examination by an opposing lawyer: While the witness is under cross-examination the lawyer ought not to have any conversation with the witness respecting the witness's evidence or relative to any issue in the proceeding.

(e) Between completion of cross-examination and commencement of re-examination the lawyer who is going to re-examine the witness ought not to have any discussion respecting evidence that will be dealt with on re-examination.

(f) During cross-examination by the lawyer of a witness unsympathetic to the cross-examiner's cause the lawyer may properly discuss the witness's evidence with the witness.

(g) During cross-examination by the lawyer of a witness who is sympathetic to that lawyer's cause any conversations ought to be restricted in the same way as communications during examination-in-chief of one's own witness.

(h) During re-examination of a witness called by an opposing lawyer: If the witness is sympathetic to the lawyer's cause there ought to be no communication relating to the evidence to be given by that witness during re-examination. The lawyer may, however, properly discuss the evidence with a witness who is adverse in interest.

If there is any question whether the lawyer's behaviour may be in violation of a rule of conduct or professional etiquette, it will often be appropriate to obtain the consent of the opposing lawyer and leave of the court before engaging in conversations that may be considered improper or a breach of etiquette.

The Lawyer as Witness

16. (a) The lawyer who appears as advocate should not submit the lawyer's own affidavit to the tribunal.

(b) The lawyer who appears as advocate should not testify before the tribunal save as may be permitted by the Rules of Civil Procedure or as to purely formal or uncontroverted matters. Nor should the lawyer express personal opinions or beliefs, or assert as a fact anything that is properly subject to legal proof, cross-examination or challenge. The lawyer must not in effect appear as an unsworn witness or put the lawyer's own credibility in issue. The lawyer who is a necessary witness should testify and entrust the conduct of the case to another lawyer. The lawyer who was a witness in the proceedings should not appear as advocate in any appeal from the decision in those proceedings. There are no restrictions on the advocate's right to cross-examine another lawyer, however, and the lawyer who does appear as a witness should not expect to receive special treatment because of professional status.

(c) The requirements of this paragraph are at all times subject to any contrary provisions of the law or the discretion of the tribunal before which the lawyer is appearing.

Ontario Labour-Management Arbitrators Association

CODE OF ETHICS*

It is the purpose and objective of the Ontario Labour-Management Arbitrators Association (the "Association") to promote policies, practices and procedures that are effective in dealing with conflicts of rights and interests in a way that is in the best interest of the parties; namely the employers, the unions and the workers. To that end, the Association has established this code of ethics (the "Code") for its members to follow in the conduct of arbitrations in the Province of Ontario and elsewhere. While the focus of the Association is on dispute resolution procedures in the labour relations sector, it is the expectation of the Association that its members will adhere to the standards and principles of conduct herein set out in all aspects of their professional activities as neutral third parties in dispute resolution procedures. Ethical standards by definition require the exercise of judgement. Membership in the Association shall constitute a Member's undertaking and covenant to abide by this Code both in letter and spirit.

Chapter I
Qualification and Professional Responsibility

Article 1. Honesty, integrity, impartiality, mutual acceptance and a general competence in labour relations matters and the law related thereto are each an essential quality required of any arbitrator. An arbitrator must at all times behave with dignity and uphold the integrity of the office.

Article 2. An arbitrator must be as ready to rule for one party as for the other on each issue, such ruling to be dependent on the merits of the particular issue only.

Article 3. An arbitrator must decline an appointment when he or she has reason to believe prior to the appointment that any matter is involved which is beyond his or her competence. If in the course of the arbitration, the arbitrator determines this to be the case, he or she must withdraw from the matter or with the consent of the parties obtain appropriate assistance.

*Adopted at the Association's annual meeting in November 1992.

Article 4.   An experienced arbitrator shall contribute to the training of new arbitrators.

Article 5.   An arbitrator must not solicit arbitration assignments. An arbitrator may make known to any party or governmental agency details as to availability if such information is requested. An arbitrator may indicate on business cards and biographical sketches or in publications accurate information as to education, professional affiliations and experience and may be listed as an arbitrator in telephone directories of general circulation. No claims of specific results or materials which imply favour of one side over another may be used or published. No commissions, rebates or other forms of remuneration may be given or received by an arbitrator for the referral of work. Advertising that is in form and substance consistent with the Code will not constitute a breach of the code.

Chapter II
Duties to the Parties

Article 6.   An arbitrator should conscientiously endeavour to understand and observe, to the extent consistent with professional responsibility, the significant principles and objectives applicable in each arbitration system in which he or she serves.

Article 7.   Before accepting any arbitration appointment, there must be full and fair disclosure to the parties by the arbitrator of any material current or past business or professional relationship or any involvement as an advisor, director or trustee, with any party to the arbitration. There must also be full and fair disclosure of any material interest which the arbitrator may have in the outcome of the arbitration, any close personal relationship to any of the parties and any other matter or consequence known to the arbitrator which would reasonably raise a question as to the arbitrator's impartiality. If after such disclosure all parties consent, the arbitrator may accept the appointment.

Article 8.   When an arbitrator is serving concurrently as an advocate for other companies or unions in labour relations matters, or has done so in recent years, such activities must be disclosed to the parties before acceptance of the appointment.

Article 9.   If in the course of an arbitration, the arbitrator becomes aware of a circumstance or matter that would have required disclosure if known prior to accepting the appointment, it must be immediately disclosed to the parties and the arbitrator may continue to act only with the consent of all parties.

Article 10.   All significant aspects of an arbitration proceeding must be treated by the arbitrator as confidential unless this requirement is waived by all parties or disclosure is required or permitted by law or established custom.

Article 11.   The arbitrator must, once the hearing of evidence and argument is completed, complete deliberations and render an award with a decision and the reasons therefor within a reasonable time; and in any event, within the time frame contemplated by the collective agreement, any applicable legislation, and any other understanding reached with the parties. If unable to comply, the arbitrator must so advise the parties in writing with the reasons for delay and request that they grant an extension of time. The arbitrator must not disclose the contents of any award prior to its simultaneous release to all parties.

Article 12.   It is a basic professional responsibility of an arbitrator to plan his or her work schedule so that present and future commitments with respect to holding hearings and rendering decisions will be fulfilled in a timely manner.

Article 13.   In the absence of an agreement by all parties, an arbitrator must provide a fair and adequate hearing in all respects consistent with the principles of natural justice and consistent with all applicable rules and procedures provided by law, which assures that all parties have sufficient opportunity to present their respective evidence and argument.

Chapter III
Fees

Article 14.   An arbitrator occupies a position of trust in respect to the parties and the administrative agencies. In charging for services and expenses, the arbitrator must be governed by the same high standards of honour and integrity that apply to all other phases of his or her work.

Article 15.   An arbitrator must endeavour to keep total charges for services and expenses reasonable and consistent with the nature of the case or cases decided.

Article 16.   Prior to appointment, the parties should be aware of or be able readily to determine all significant aspects of an arbitrator's bases for charges for fees and expenses.

Article 17.   An arbitrator must render accounts and charge for services strictly in accordance with any procedures adopted by the Association. In the event of any fee dispute, the arbitrator must agree to be bound by any decision reached pursuant to the Fees Mediation Service operated by the Association, If the other parties to the fee dispute also agree to be bound.

Chapter IV
Ethics and Professional Responsibility Committee

Article 18   Any complaint by a party to an arbitration against the arbitrator involved that the arbitrator has not acted in conformity with the provisions of this Code must be submitted in writing to the Secretary of the Association, who will decide whether or not there are grounds to refer it to the Committee. If the secretary believes there are not grounds, the complainant will be notified in writing with the secretary's reasons succinctly stated. If the complainant advises the secretary the reasons are not satisfactory, the complaint will be referred to the Committee.

Article 19   The Committee will be comprised of the President of the Association, a member of the Association Executive designated by the President and a member of the Association designated by the complainant. If the complainant fails to designate such a member within 15 days of being notified in writing to make such designation, then the third member of the committee will be designated by the President.

Article 20   The Committee so constituted shall conduct such inquiries and make such investigations as it considers reasonable and consistent with principles of due process and natural justice. The Committee will decide whether the complaint was justified and may make recommendations to the Association. The Committee will try to reach a unanimous report to the Association, but if unable to do so, the members will make their individual recommendations. The complainant and the arbitrator will be entitled to receive copies of any reports and recommendations made by the Committee or its members.

Article 21   If the Committee or a majority of its members so recommend, the membership in the Association of an arbitrator, against whom a complaint is found to be justified, may be suspended for such period as the Committee or a majority of its members consider to be appropriate, or the Committee may issue such reprimand to the arbitrator as the Committee considers appropriate.

Article 22   A Committee comprising any three members of the Executive of the Association designated by the President may be constituted at any time to consider any issue or question posed by anyone relative to the arbitration process and the role of an arbitrator therein. The Committee so constituted shall make such inquiry and investigations as it deems necessary and may if it considers it appropriate issue and advisory opinion on the question.

Excerpt from *United Brotherhood of Carpenters and Joiners of America, Local 579 v. Bradco Construction Ltd.*

(1993), 102 D.L.R. (4th) 402

Supreme Court of Canada, May 19, 1993

MR. JUSTICE SOPINKA:

Section 84(1) of the *Labour Relations Act, 1977* provides that the arbitrator may receive and accept such evidence as he deems advisable whether or not it would be admissible in a court of law. By s. 84(1), the legislator has specifically indicated that the arbitrator need not concern himself with the common law rules governing the admission of extrinsic evidence, including the debate as to whether an ambiguity need be patent or latent or even exists at all. In dealing with a similar provision in the Ontario *Labour Relations Act*, the Ontario Court of Appeal stated in *Re Noranda Metal Industries Ltd., Fergus Division and I.B.E.W., Local 2345* (1983), 84 C.L.L.C. ¶14,024, 44 O.R. (2d) 529, 23 A.C.W.S. (2d) 136, that the provision was designed "to permit an arbitrator to rely on relevant evidence even where such evidence is not admissible in a court of law" (p. 12,098). While provisions such as these do not oust judicial review completely, they enable the arbitrator to relax the rules of evidence. This reflects the fact that arbitrators are often not trained in the law and are permitted to apply the rules in the same way as would be done by reasonable persons in the conduct of their business. Section 84(1) evinces a legislative intent to leave these matters to the decision of the arbitrator. Accordingly, an arbitrator's decision in this regard is not reviewable unless it is shown to be patently unreasonable. While failure to give effect to a rule of privilege or an exclusionary rule of evidence which embodies an important aspect of public policy might, without more, attract review, the use of extrinsic evidence to interpret a collective agreement is very much in the core area of an arbitrator's function. In this regard, the court is not apt to intervene provided the approach adopted by the arbitrator with respect to the use to be made of the evidence assists in determining the true intention of the parties.

Syndicat des employés professionnels de l'Université du Québec à Trois-Rivières v. Université du Québec à Trois-Rivières

(1993), 101 D.L.R. (4th) 494

Supreme Court of Canada, February 25, 1993

CHIEF JUSTICE LAMER:

Facts

In October, 1985, an agreement was concluded between the Government of Quebec and the respondent Université du Québec à Trois-Rivières whereby research was to be conducted by the respondent by means of questionnaires and interviews. The agreement provided for an initial payment of $25,000 on the signing of the agreement and a second payment of $33,000 after the questionnaire and the interview plan were submitted. A committee was set up under the authority of the director of research at the Ministère de l'éducation to provide follow-up on the research. Responsibility for the work was assigned to Professor Jean-Luc Gouvéia, who hired the mis en cause Perreault and Guilbert as grant-aided part-time professional research assistants. The date the employment commenced was to be October 15, 1985, and its termination December 15, 1986 (translation) "or on notice from the University for cause".

An initial working document prepared by the mis en cause was submitted to the follow-up committee on or about April 15, 1986. This presentation was behind the schedule specified in the agreement between the government and the respondent.

On May 1, 1986, the respondent advised the mis en cause by letter that (translation) "as the result of a lack of funds" it would be forced to terminate their contract as of April 25, 1986.

A grievance was then filed for each of the mis en cause and at the first arbitration hearing, the respondent contended that the arbitrator lacked jurisdiction by alleging that the grievance could not be arbitrated under the collective agreement. This allegation was dismissed by the mis en cause arbitrator in a preliminary decision dated December 16, 1986.

In February, 1987, the mis en cause arbitrator proceeded to hear the grievances on the merits. The respondent then sought to introduce evidence that the two mis en cause employees had done their work badly and that, accordingly, in order to meet the schedule agreed on in the contract between the government and the respondent, it was necessary to hire from the research funds another experienced person who would be able to redo the work done by the mis en cause in April, 1986, and found by the government's representatives to be of poor quality. It is this additional expenditure which, on the evidence which the respondent sought to present, led to the shortage of funds to pay the two assistants.

The appellant objected to this evidence on the ground that the respondent was trying to add to or alter the grounds relied on in the notices of termination of employment of May 1, 1986. The appellant contended that the respondent wanted to present evidence on the competence of the two mis en cause professionals when the sole and exclusive reason given by the respondent for ordering the termination of employment was a lack of funds. The mis en cause arbitrator allowed the appellant's objection. On March 19, 1987, he made an award allowing the two grievances and ordering the respondent to pay the mis en cause their full salary.

The respondent then submitted a motion in evocation to the Superior Court, alleging first that the arbitrator had assumed jurisdiction which he did not have in deciding that the mis en cause benefited from the grievance procedure laid down in the collective agreement. Alternatively, it argued that the arbitrator had exceeded his jurisdiction by not admitting evidence of the lack of competence of the two mis en cause. The Superior Court allowed the motion, rejecting the respondent's arguments as to the arbitrator's jurisdiction to hear the grievances but finding that his refusal to hear the evidence offered by the respondent constituted an excess of jurisdiction. It ordered that the case be reheard before another arbitrator.

The appellant appealed the part of the judgment vacating the arbitral award and ordering a new arbitration. The respondent then filed a cross-appeal, challenging the other part of the judgement which recognized the arbitrator's jurisdiction to hear the grievances filed by the mis en cause. On August 21, 1990, the Court of Appeal dismissed the two appeals, Rousseau-Houle J.A. dissenting on the main appeal. The present appeal is from the Court of Appeal's judgment on the main appeal.

Applicable legislation

Section 100.2 of the *Labour Code*, R.S.Q., c. C-27, reads as follows:

> 100.2 The arbitrator shall proceed with all dispatch with the inquiry into the grievance and, unless otherwise provided in the collective agreement, in accordance with such procedure and mode of proof as he deems appropriate.
>
> For such purpose, he may, *ex officio*, call the parties to proceed with the hearing of the grievance.

Applicable provisions of the collective agreement

Clauses 2-1.03(A), 5-1.01 and 5-5.01 of the collective agreement read as follows (translation):

> 2-1.03(A) A supernumerary, temporary, replacement or grant-aided professional is subject to the following provisions:

• • • • •

(5) Hiring, probation, resignation (article 5-1.00), except for clauses 5-1.03, 5-1.04 and 5-1.05.

⁙ ⁙ ⁙ ⁙ ⁙

(19) Procedure for the settlement of grievances and disputes and arbitration (chapter 11-0.00) to claim the benefits conferred herein.

⁙ ⁙ ⁙ ⁙ ⁙

5-1.01 All professionals shall be hired by a contract which the personnel branch will deliver to the professional, indicating to him certain of his terms and conditions of employment (group, classification, salary, date of hiring, probation period, probable length of employment in the case of a supernumerary, temporary, replacement, grant-aided or casual professional). A copy of this contract shall be sent to the union when the professional commences his or her employment.

5-5.01(a) When an act done by a professional leads to disciplinary action the University, depending on the seriousness of the alleged act, shall take one of the following three (3) steps:
–written warning;
–suspension;
–dismissal.

(b) The University shall inform the professional in writing that he or she is subject to disciplinary action within twenty (20) working days of the time the University becomes aware of the offence alleged against him or her: this is a strict time limit and the burden of proof of subsequent knowledge of the facts by the University is on the University.

(c) In all cases in which the University takes disciplinary action, the professional concerned or the Union may have recourse to the grievance and arbitration procedure; the burden of proof that the cause in question is just and sufficient for disciplinary action to be taken is on the University.

(d) In the event that the University wishes to take disciplinary action against a professional, it shall summon the said professional by at least twenty-four (24) hours' written notice; at the same time, the University shall advise the Union that the professional has been summoned.

(e) The notice sent to the professional shall specify the time and place at which he shall attend and the nature of the facts alleged against him. The professional may be accompanied by a union representative.

Judgments

Arbitration tribunal—preliminary decision

In the preliminary decision of December 16, 1986, the arbitrator held that he had total, absolute and exclusive jurisdiction to hear and decide the grievances presented by the complainants. He accordingly dismissed the objection made by counsel for the university that the dismissal of the grant-aided professionals was not subject to arbitration. The arbitrator pointed out that cl. 2-1.03(A) of the collective agreement, governing grant-aided professionals, makes them subject to the grievance procedure in claiming the benefits conferred by the collective agreement. Clause 5-1.01 provides that the hiring of any professional shall be by contract and that this contract shall specify, *inter alia*, the group, classification, salary, date of hiring, probation period and probable length of the employment in the case of a grant-aided professional. According to the arbitrator, it follows that if there is disagreement as to the interpretation or application of any of the provisions of the hiring contract, that disagreement is a grievance within the meaning of the Act and the collective agreement. The arbitrator stated that the contrary solution, namely referring complainants to proceedings in the ordinary courts of law, would be contrary to the manifest intention of the legislature that all grievances be subject to arbitration. This solution would also, the arbitrator concluded, be contrary to the spirit of the Supreme Court decision in *St. Anne-Nackawic Pulp & Paper Co. v. C.P.U., Local 219* (1986), 28 D.L.R. (4th) 1, [1986] 1 S.C.R. 704, 86 C.L.L.C. ¶14,037. Finally, the arbitrator stated that there would have to be a very clear provision to exempt a privilege conferred under a collective labour agreement from the arbitration mechanism provided for in the event of a dispute.

Arbitration tribunal—decision on the merits

In his decision on the merits of the grievances rendered on March 19, 1987, the arbitrator first stated that when the university referred to a lack of funds, it could only mean funds of the employer, the Université du Québec à Trois-Rivières, with which the complainants had entered into a contract. He noted that the university had the burden of establishing the lack of funds and found that the university had not succeeded in showing that it lacked funds to pay the two employees up to the date of termination provided for in the contract. He observed that there was no evidence that the government had broken its contract with the university and indicated that the university was under no obligation to offer 14-month contracts. He concluded that the university had not discharged its burden of proving the lack of funds and that accordingly there was no cause for interrupting the contracts.

The arbitrator added that even if there had been a lack of funds, that lack could not be a valid reason for breaching a term contract, since (translation) "[i]t is a cause which is not within the employee's control, but due to an agreement between the University and a third party". He stated that, in cases of dismissal for cause in the context of term contracts, the authors and cases require that the employer establish a breach of an essential condition of the contract of employment, a breach for which the employee is responsible. This is why he found that a (translation) "… fact beyond the employee's control, such as the non-payment of money by a third party to the employer, and indeed the employer's poor economic situation, cannot be a cause for the breach of a contract of employment that relieves the employer of its obligations".

Superior Court

On the question of the arbitrator's jurisdiction Lebrun J., after recalling the principles set out by the Supreme Court in *St. Anne-Nackawic Pulp & Paper, supra,* and listing the provisions of the collective agreement in effect between the parties and applicable to the complainants, held that (translation):

> In deciding to hear the grievance, the respondent arbitrator applied what I would call the presumption that a grievance is arbitrable when, as here, everything tends to show that the individual contract of the parties is clearly subject to the provisions of the collective agreement and therefore to the arbitration mechanisms provided for therein.

However, Lebrun J. accepted the respondent's alternative argument. Referring to the arbitral award, he noted that the arbitrator had confined his ruling to the contractual relationship between the respondent and the mis en cause in deciding on the merits of the grievance and had refused to hear the evidence that the reason the respondent lacked funds was precisely the poor quality of the work done by the mis en cause. Accordingly, he was of the view that (translation):

> On the one hand, by blaming [the respondent] for not establishing that the cause of dismissal was something for which the mis en cause employees were responsible, and on the other, by denying [the respondent] the opportunity to establish that very fact based on a narrow interpretation of the "cause" of dismissal, the [mis en cause] arbitrator was refusing to hear admissible and relevant evidence ...

Relying on the Supreme Court judgment in *Roberval Express Ltd. v. Transport Drivers, Warehousemen and General Workers Union, Local 106* (1982), 144 D.L.R. (3d) 673, [1982] 2 S.C.R. 888, 83 C.L.L.C. ¶14,023, the judge concluded that the arbitrator had exceeded his jurisdiction by refusing to hear relevant and admissible evidence.

Court of Appeal, [1990] R.J.Q. 2183, 22 A.C.W.S. (3d) 809

Baudouin J.A.

On the question of the arbitrator's jurisdiction, Baudouin J.A. agreed that the relevant provisions of the collective agreement were not "crystal clear". However, he held that this document should be read as a whole and its purposes taken into account. He also referred to the general philosophy of Quebec labour law and concluded that the arbitrator had jurisdiction to decide the two grievances and so had not arrogated to himself jurisdiction exercisable only by the ordinary courts of law.

On the second issue, Baudouin J.A., for the majority, upheld the Superior Court's decision that the arbitrator had exceeded his jurisdiction. Noting first that the Superior Court had found in the respondent's favour mainly owing to the fact that the arbitrator had not observed the *audi alteram partem* rule, the judge went on to say (at p. 2187) (translation):

> With all due respect, it does not seems to me that that resolves the problem. It is still necessary to determine whether this evidence was relevant and admissible. There does not seem to be any doubt as to the relevance of the evidence, since it seeks to establish that the need to terminate the employment before the time

specified was caused by what the two research assistants themselves did. I am of the view that its admissibility results from the
very interpretation of the collective agreement between the parties. No provision is to be found in that agreement requiring the
employer in cases of grant-aided professionals ... to give the facts
or reasons behind the dismissal. On the contrary, article 2-1.03
expressly excludes the application to this class of employees of
clause 5-5.01 requiring the employer to do that. The university
accordingly had no contractual obligation to give in writing the
specific reasons for terminating the employment, subject to not
being able to rely on them in the event of arbitration. The allegation
of lack of funds was sufficient. Evidence of the reasons for this lack
of funds was nonetheless not irrelevant or inadmissible.

Rousseau-Houle J.A. (dissenting on the main appeal)

Rousseau-Houle J.A. concurred with the reasons of Baudouin J.A. regarding the arbitrator's jurisdiction. However, she was of the view that the
arbitrator had not exceeded his jurisdiction in not admitting evidence of the
poor quality of the work done by the mis en cause employees.

Rousseau-Houle J.A. held that under s. 100.2 of the *Labour Code*, it is up
to the arbitrator to decide on the relevance and admissibility of the evidence
the parties intend to submit. His decisions are thus subject to judicial review
only if there is a breach of nature justice or patently unreasonable error.

The judge considered that the respondent had been allowed to present
argument on the lack of funds and that it had only been prevented from
establishing another ground of dismissal, namely the incompetence of the
research assistants, a ground which it had not mentioned in the employment
termination notices.

Bearing in mind the limited purpose of the arbitrator's jurisdiction, namely
to hear and decide the grievance before him, the judge was of the view that the
arbitrator (translation) "may consider the notion of relevance of the evidence
more narrowly than a judge would when hearing witnesses" (p. 2188). She
noted that the dispute submitted to the arbitrator here concerned the probable
length of the contracts hiring the two mis en cause employees and the reason
given by the respondent for terminating them.

The judge considered that the arbitrator's decision to refuse to admit the
evidence on the ground that the respondent was actually trying to prove a cause
of dismissal not mentioned in the notices was not unreasonable. She went on
to say (at p. 2189) (translation):

> That decision does not seem arbitrary or illogical to me either,
> since it was a necessary part of determining the point at issue and
> noted that there was not really an adequate connection between
> that point and the evidence presented.

• • • • •

In adopting a strict interpretation of the cause of dismissal, rather than granting an adjournment or admitting the evidence under advisement, the arbitrator did not exercise his jurisdiction unreasonably.

The judge further held that the arbitrator's refusal to allow the evidence also should not be regarded as a refusal to exercise his jurisdiction contrary to the rules of natural justice, since it is only a refusal to hear relevant and admissible evidence which constitutes an excess of jurisdiction. She felt that the respondent here had had an opportunity to put forward evidence regarding the lack of funds. She noted that the arbitrator had to reconcile the demands of the decision-making process with the rights of all parties and pointed out that the *audi alteram partem* rule was intended essentially to give the parties a reasonable opportunity to respond to the evidence presented against them.

Issues

Though the appellant formulated six questions, in my opinion, this appeal really only raises two. First, it must be determined whether the refusal by a grievance arbitrator to admit evidence is a decision subject to judicial review, and in particular whether the Superior Court was justified in exercising its review power in the case at bar. Secondly, the court must decide whether the Superior Court erred in ordering that the new arbitration hearing would be before another arbitrator.

Analysis

(a) Refusal to admit evidence and judicial review

The question therefore is whether, in deciding not to admit the evidence offered by the respondent, the arbitrator committed an error giving rise to judicial review. In their consideration of this question, Lebrun J. of the Superior Court and Baudouin J.A. speaking for the majority of the Court of Appeal both referred to the following passage from Chouinard J.'s judgment in *Roberval Express, supra*, at p. 685: "Appellant alleged a refusal by the arbitrator to hear admissible and relevant evidence. A refusal to hear admissible and relevant evidence is so clear a case of excess or refusal to exercise jurisdiction that it needs no further comment."

It should be noted, however, that *Roberval Express* did not involve a simple refusal by a grievance arbitrator to hear relevant evidence. The arbitrator, who was to hear four grievances, had refused to hear the first three and heard only the grievance relating to the dismissal of the employee in question. The first three grievances concerned disciplinary action leading up to that dismissal. The employer contended that the dismissal resulted from incidents which gave rise to the disciplinary action and it was therefore necessary to hear all the grievances at the same time. Accordingly, it attacked the arbitrator not only for not hearing certain evidence, but more importantly, for refusing to exercise his jurisdiction over three of the grievances presented to him.

When thus seen in their context it is not clear that Chouinard J.'s remarks can be used to dispose of this case. Accordingly, this court must examine the question presented to it on the basis of the particular circumstances of this case, the arguments made by the parties and the general principles governing judicial review in the field of grievance arbitration.

(i) Determining the scope of this case

The appellant first argued that the present appeal actually concerns not the mis en cause arbitrator's failure to admit the evidence submitted by the respondent, but the mis en cause arbitrator's understanding of the issue presented to him, a question over which the grievance arbitrator has exclusive jurisdiction, free from judicial review except in the case of a patently unreasonable error or a breach of natural justice. In other words, the appellant argued that the exclusion of the evidence resulted here from the mis en cause arbitrator's decision to confine himself to the cause mentioned in the notice of dismissal and that that decision could only be reversed once it was shown to be patently unreasonable or a breach of natural justice.

As far as this argument is concerned, in my opinion, there is no doubt that the mis en cause arbitrator had complete jurisdiction to define the scope of the issue presented to him and that in this regard only a patently unreasonable error or a breach of natural justice could give rise to judicial review. The question is in no way one which could be characterized as jurisdictional in nature.

For some years, since the decision of Dickson J. in *C.U.P.E., Local 963 v. New Brunswick Liquor Corp.* (1979), 97 D.L.R. (3d) 417, [1979] 2 S.C.R. 227, 79 C.L.LC. ¶14,209, this court has made an effort to limit the scope of the theory of preliminary questions. In *U.E.S., Local 298 v. Bibeault*, [1988] 2 S.C.R. 1048, 35 Admin. L.R. 153, 89 C.L.L.C. ¶14,045, *sub nom. Syndicat National des Employés de la Commission Scolaire Régionale de l'Outaouais v. Union des Employés de Service, Local 298*, Beetz J. favoured instead a functional and pragmatic approach to identifying questions of jurisdiction. He said (at p. 1087):

> The concept of the preliminary or collateral question diverts the courts from the real problem of judicial review: it substitutes the question "Is this a preliminary or collateral question to the exercise of the tribunal's power?" for the only question which should be asked, "Did the legislator intend the question to be within the jurisdiction conferred on the tribunal?"

Applying this approach to the question of the grievance arbitrator's jurisdiction to define the scope of the issue presented to him, I am unable to conclude that the legislature intended such a matter to be beyond the arbitrator's exclusive jurisdiction. This is especially true in the instant case in that in order to determine the scope of the issue presented to him the arbitrator had primarily to interpret the collective agreement, the contracts concluded between the mis en cause Perreault and Guilbert and the respondent—contracts covered by cl. 5-1.01 of the collective agreement—and the wording of the grievances filed by the appellant. Interpretation of such documents is clearly within the grievance arbitrator's exclusive jurisdiction.

This approach may seem to be at odds with the decision of this court in *Toronto Newspaper Guild v. Globe Printing Co.*, [1953] 3 D.L.R. 561, 106 C.C.C. 225, [1953] 2 S.C.R. 18. In that case, which also involved the exclusion of evidence, Kerwin J. suggested that, far from being non-reviewable by the courts, the error of an administrative tribunal in determining the questions which were the subject of its inquiry was on the contrary, depending on whether the tribunal was wrongly refusing to examine a question or concerning itself with a question not presented to it, a refusal by that tribunal to exercise its jurisdiction or an excess of jurisdiction justifying intervention by the courts.

This judgment, however, may be classified among the decisions of this court which, as Wilson J. noted in *National Corn Growers Assn. v. Canada (Canadian Import Tribunal)* (1990), 74 D.L.R. (4th) 449, [1990] 2 S.C.R. 1324, 45 Admin. L.R. 161, demonstrates the reluctance Canadian courts had long shown "... to accept the proposition that tribunals should not be subject to the same standard of review as courts" (p. 455). As Wilson J. explained, administrative law has developed considerably since that time, so that courts of law now allow administrative tribunals much greater independence. *New Brunswick Liquor Corp., supra*, represents the culmination of this development.

In view of the foregoing, I have no hesitation in concluding that the arbitrator had complete jurisdiction to define the scope of the issue presented to him and that only an unreasonable error on his part in this regard or a breach of natural justice could have constituted an excess of jurisdiction. I also think, though in my opinion it is not necessary to decide this point in the case at bar, that the necessary corollary of the grievance arbitrator's exclusive jurisdiction to define the issue is his exclusive jurisdiction then to conduct the proceedings accordingly, and that he may, *inter alia*, choose to admit only the evidence he considers relevant to the case as he has chosen to define it.

In my opinion, however, these comments do not dispose of the case at bar. The respondent is not complaining only, or even primarily, of the fact that in refusing to admit the evidence it had to offer the arbitrator erred in understanding the issue presented to him. Rather, it is arguing that even within the issue as defined by the arbitrator—that is, an issue limited to the cause relied on in the notices of dismissal, the lack of funds—this evidence was relevant since its very purpose was to establish the reason for this lack of funds. It maintained that the refusal to admit relevant and admissible evidence infringes the rules of natural justice and for that reason constitutes an excess of jurisdiction.

In other words, the question now before this court is not whether, after deciding wrongly but not unreasonably that he should limit his analysis to a single ground of dismissal, an arbitrator who then decides to exclude evidence of other possible reasons for dismissal commits an error that is beyond judicial review by the courts. The answer to this question is simple: it is yes. The arbitrator is then acting within his jurisdiction.

The question before this court is instead whether, in erroneously deciding to exclude evidence relevant to the ground of dismissal which he has himself identified as being that which he must examine, the arbitrator *necessarily* commits an excess of jurisdiction. In my view, the anwser to this question must in general be no. It will be yes, however, if by his erroneous decision the arbitrator was led to infringe the rules of natural justice. I therefore now turn to considering this question.

(ii) Refusal to admit relevant evidence and natural justice

The only rule of natural justice with which the court is concerned here is the right of a person affected by a decision to be heard, that is, the *audi alteram partem* rule. The question is whether there is a breach of that rule whenever relevant evidence is rejected by a grievance arbitrator. In order to answer this question, we must determine whether judicial review should be available whenever an arbitrator errs, regardless of the seriousness of his error, in declaring evidence submitted by the parties to be irrelevant or inadmissible.

The difficulty of this question arises from the tension existing between the quest for effectiveness and speed in settling grievances on the one hand, and on the other preserving the credibility of the arbitration process, which depends on the parties' believing that they have had a complete opportunity to be heard. Professor Ouellette speaks in this regard of the (translation) "... perpetual contradiction between freedom of operation and its necessary procedural aspects": Yves Ouellette, "Aspects de la procédure et de la preuve devant les tribunaux administratifs" (1986), 16 R.D.U.S. 819 at p. 850. Professor Evans also states:

> There is a certain tension between the proposition that an administrative tribunal, even if required to hold an adjudicative-type hearing, is not bound by the whole body of the law of evidence applied in proceedings in courts of law, and the imposition of a duty to decide in a procedurally fair manner.

(J.M. Evans *et al., Administrative Law*, 3rd ed. (Toronto: Emond Montgomery Publications Ltd., 1989) at p. 452.)

For this reason, the question before the court cannot simply be answered, as the appellant suggests, by reference to s. 100.2 of the *Labour Code*, which provides:

Inquiry into grievance

> 100.2 The arbitrator shall proceed with all dispatch with the inquiry into the grievance and, unless otherwise provided in the collective agreement, in accordance with such procedure and mode of proof as he deems appropriate.

The appellant argued that this provision gave a grievance arbitrator exclusive jurisdiction to decide on the relevance of the evidence presented to him and that his decisions in this regard are consequently beyond the scope of judicial review except in the event of patently unreasonable error.

This argument cannot be accepted. Section 100.2 of the *Labour Code* does give a grievance arbitrator complete autonomy in dealing with points of evidence and procedure; but the rule of autonomy in administrative procedure and evidence, widely accepted in administrative law, has never had the effect of limiting the obligation on administrative tribunals to observe the requirements of natural justice. This is what Professor Ouellette says in this regard, *supra*, at p. 850 (translation):

> ... the major decisions which formulated the principle of the independence of administrative evidence from technical rules have in the same breath made it clear that this independence must be exercised in accordance with the rules of fundamental justice. It is not sufficient for administrative tribunals to operate simply and effectively: they must attain this high ideal without sacrificing the fundamental rights of the parties.

It is true that the error of an administrative tribunal in determining the relevance of evidence is an error of law and that in general the decisions of administrative tribunals which enjoy the protection of a complete privative clause are beyond judicial review for mere errors of law.

That is not true, however, in cases where, as occurred here in the submission of the respondent, the arbitrator's decision on the relevance of evidence had the effect of breaching the rules of natural justice. A breach of the rules of natural justice is regarded in itself as an excess of jurisdiction and consequently there is no doubt that such a breach opens the way for judicial review; but that brings us back to the point at issue in this case: was there a breach of natural justice as a result of the mis en cause arbitrator's refusal to admit the evidence submitted by the respondent?

The proposition that any refusal to admit relevant evidence is in the context of a grievance arbitration a breach of natural justice is one which could have serious consequences. It in effect means that the arbitrator does not have the power to decide in a final and exclusive way what evidence will be relevant to the issue presented to him. That may seem incompatible with the very wide measure of autonomy which the legislature intended to give grievance arbitrators in settling disputes within their jurisdiction and the attitude of restraint demonstrated by the courts toward the decisions of administrative bodies.

At the same time, it is clear that the confidence of the parties bound by the final decisions of grievance arbitrators is likely to be undermined by the reckless rejection of relevant evidence. A certain caution is therefore unquestionably necessary in this regard. As Professor Garant observes (translation):

> A tribunal must be cautious, however, as it is much more serious to refuse to admit relevant evidence than to admit irrelevant evidence, which may later be rejected in the final decision. The practice of a tribunal taking objections to evidence "under advisement" where possible, and when the party making them does not absolutely insist on having a decision right then, is usually advisable; it does not in any way contravene natural justice.

(Patrice Garante, *Droit administratif*, vol. 2: *Le contentieux*, 3rd ed. (Cowansville: Yvon Blais, 1991), at p. 231.)

For my part, I am not prepared to say that the rejection of relevant evidence is automatically a breach of natural justice. A grievance arbitrator is in a privileged position to assess the relevance of evidence presented to him and I do not think it is desirable for the courts, in the guise of protecting the right of parties to be heard, to substitute their own assessment of the evidence for that of the grievance arbitrator. It may happen, however, that the rejection of relevant evidence has such an impact on the fairness of the proceeding, leading unavoidably to the conclusion that there has been a breach of natural justice.

Accordingly, in the case before the court there is no doubt, in my opinion, that there was a breach of natural justice. The respondent wished to present evidence of the poor quality of the work of the mis en cause, Perreault and Guilbert. It sought to show that as a consequence of the poor quality of their work it had been forced to obtain other resources in order to meet the requirements of the granting organization and that accordingly not enough money remained from the grant to pay the salaries of the mis en cause. In the context of a hearing involving a dismissal due to a lack of funds, such evidence is *prima facie* crucial. Its purpose is to establish the cause of the lack of funds. If there are still any doubts as to the significance of this evidence, they are dispelled by the following remarks by the mis en cause arbitrator (translation): "Even if there was a lack of funds, that lack could not be a valid reason for breaking a term contract. It is a cause which is not within the employee's control, but is due to an agreement between the University and a third party."

In light of these remarks by the mis en cause arbitrator, one can only conclude that there was a breach of natural justice. As Lebrun J. pointed out, the mis en cause arbitrator adopted a paradoxical position (translation):

On the one hand, by blaming [the respondent] for not establishing that the cause of the dismissal was something for which the mis en cause employees were responsible, and on the other, by denying [the respondent] the opportunity to establish that very fact based on a narrow interpretation of the "cause" of dismissal ...

The consequence of this paradoxical position taken by the mis en cause arbitrator is that he found himself in the position of disposing of an extremely important point in the case before him—namely the lack of cause attributable to the employees—without having heard *any evidence whatever* from the respondent on the point, and even having expressly refused to hear the evidence which the respondent sought to present on the point. This quite clearly amounts to a breach of natural justice.

The appellant argued that the arbitrator's comments on the lack of any cause attributable to the mis en cause were only obiter and that the arbitrator would quite clearly have come to the same decision even if he had heard the evidence the respondent was seeking to present. It contended that the real reason for the arbitrator's decision was that the lack of funds itself had not been established in this case and moreover could never be a valid cause for dismissal.

This argument cannot be accepted. First, it is impossible to say with any certainty what the decision of the mis en cause arbitrator would have been if he had heard the evidence offered by the respondent. That evidence might have convinced him that in the particular circumstances of this case, and especially in view of the relationship existing between the respondent and the granting organization, the lack of funds could be a cause for dismissal attributable to the fault of the employees and that this ground could accordingly justify the respondent in terminating the employment contracts.

Secondly, and more fundamentally, the rules of natural justice have enshrined certain guarantees regarding procedure and it is the denial of those procedural guarantees which justifies the courts in intervening. The application of these rules should thus not depend on speculation as to what the decision on the merits would have been had the rights of the parties not been denied. I concur in this regard with the view of Le Dain J., who stated in *Cardinal v. Kent Institution (Director)* (1985), 24 D.L.R. (4TH) 44 at p. 57, 23 C.C.C. (3d) 118, [1985] 2 S.C.R. 643:

> ... the denial of a right to a fair hearing must always render a decision invalid, whether or not it may appear to a reviewing court that the hearing would likely have resulted in a different decision. The right to a fair hearing must be regarded as an independent, unqualified right which finds its essential justification in the sense of procedural justice which any person affected by an administrative decision is entitled to have.

For all these reasons, I conclude that by refusing to admit the evidence which the respondent was seeking to present the mis en cause arbitrator infringed the rules of natural justice. The Superior Court therefore did not err in ordering a new arbitration. Did the Superior Court, however, err in ordering that the new arbitration be held before another arbitrator?

(b) Referral of case to another arbitrator

The appellant contended that the Superior Court had erred in ordering that the new arbitration be held before another arbitrator, since there was no real, objective reason for doubting the impartiality of the mis en cause arbitrator.

On this point, in my opinion, the appellant did not succeed in establishing that the Superior Court had erred in the exercise of its discretion so as to justify intervention by this court. Though he did not actually say so, Lebrun J. was probably of the view that there could quite reasonably be doubt as to the ability of a grievance arbitrator to objectively hear evidence which he already thought was so lacking in significance as to declare it irrelevant.

Conclusion

For these reasons, the appeal is dismissed with costs.

Justices LAFOREST, GONTHIER and IACOBUCCI concur with CHIEF JUSTICE LAMER.

JUSTICE L'HEUREUX-DUBÉ—I agree entirely with the Chief Justice on the outcome of this case. However, I would adopt the approach taken by the trial judge, Guy Lebrun J., and by Baudouin J.A. for the majority of the Court of Appeal, [1990] R.J.Q. 2183, 22 A.C.W.S. (3d) 809.

When faced with a privative clause an appellate court will be held to a high standard of deference toward an administrative tribunal. However, an error on a question of law which goes to jurisdiction will always be reviewable: see *Canada (Attorney-General) v. Mossop*, S.C.C., No. 22145, judgment released on February 25, 1993, not yet reported, and the decisions cited therein) [now reported 100 D.L.R. (4th) 658, [1993] 1 S.C.R. 554, 93 C.L.L.C. ¶17,006].

Although the arbitrator in the case at bar had jurisdiction to dispose of the grievances before him, as the lower courts correctly held, he could not in so doing commit an excess of jurisdiction. In *S.E.I.U., Local 333 v. Nipawin District Staff Nurses Assn.* (1973), 41 D.L.R. (3d) 6, [1975] 1 S.C.R. 382, [1974] 1 W.W.R. 653, Dickson J. (as he then was), speaking for the court, made this point very clearly (at pp. 11-12):

> *A tribunal may, on the one hand, have jurisdiction in the narrow sense of authority to enter upon an inquiry but, in the course of that inquiry, do something which take the exercise of its powers outside the protection of the privative or preclusive clause. Examples of this type of error would include* acting in bad faith, basing the decision on extraneous matters, failing to take relevant factors into account, *breaching the provisions of natural justice* or misinterpreting provisions of the Act so as to embark on an inquiry or answer a question not remitted to it.

(Emphasis added.)

Refusing to hear relevant and admissible evidence is a breach of the rules of natural justice. It is one thing to adopt special rules of procedure for a hearing, and another not to comply with a fundamental rule, that of doing justice to the parties by hearing relevant and therefore admissible evidence. That is the case here.

In my view, the formalism and inflexibility demonstrated by the arbitrator in this case have no place in the hearing of a grievance. If the arbitrator had doubts as to the relevancy of the evidence sought to be introduced, he could have taken it under advisement as courts regularly do. This would have facilitated and speeded up the hearing. Furthermore, as is often the case, the relevance or otherwise of the evidence in question would have become apparent during the proceedings. In these circumstances, the ends of justice would have been better served for all the parties involved.

In any event, I subscribe entirely to the reasons of the majority of the Court of Appeal that the evidence presented by the respondent was relevant to the consideration and disposition of the grievances before the arbitrator. The arbitrator's refusal to consider such evidence was an excess of jurisdiction.

For these reasons, I would dispose of the appeal as the Chief Justice suggests, with costs.

GLOSSARY OF ARBITRATION TERMS

Glossary of Arbitration Terms

(from Labour Law Terms, Lancaster House)

abandon surrender interests, rights or property; e.g. by its intentional failure to process the grievance, the union has abandoned its right to proceed to arbitration

adduce present, introduce, put forward, offer; usually used in connection with evidence

ad hoc literally, for this purpose; for a specific or special purpose; arbitrators in the private sector in Ontario are generally not appointed permanently, rather they are chosen by the parties (or, in the case of expedited arbitration, selected by the Minister of Labour) on an *ad hoc* basis to deal with particular grievances

adjournment postponement or suspension, as of a hearing; an adjournment *sine die* is an adjournment without a specific date fixed for resumption

adjudicate decide, determine; the term **adjudication** is used generally to describe the determination of a dispute by a tribunal or a court, and particularly to designate the grievance arbitration process in the federal public service

admissible evidence evidence which may lawfully be adduced before a court or tribunal; the general test of admissibility is relevance, but not all relevant evidence is admissible; e.g. hearsay, even where relevant, is generally not admissible

admission acknowledgment; statement by a party, oral, written or inferred from conduct, made against its own interest or acknowledging wrongdoing, and thus admissible as evidence, even though otherwise hearsay; e.g. "the supervisor told me that he had struck the grievor first"

adverse unfavourable, opposed (in interest); e.g. the grievor's interests were adversely affected by the award of the vacancy to a junior employee

adverse inference unfavourable inference; an adverse inference may be drawn from a failure to call a material witness, that the testimony, had it been given, would not have supported the position of the party which failed to call that witness

adverse witness witness who takes a position opposed in interest to the party calling him or her and who is hostile or evasive, or has made prior statements which are contradictory; a witness declared adverse by a court or tribunal may be cross-examined by the party calling the witness; see **hostile witness**

adviser individual involved in arbitration proceedings who assists or advises the advocate who presents the case; ordinarily an adviser is permitted to remain present during a hearing, and also testify, despite an order excluding witnesses; see **exclusion of witnesses**

advocate individual, layperson or lawyer, who advances the cause of another; **advocacy** is sometimes referred to as the art of persuasion

agreed statement of facts statement of facts agreed to by both parties, which is presented to an arbitrator, so that it is not necessary to adduce evidence

aids to interpretation sources which assist an arbitrator to determine the meaning of language in statutes or documents such as collective agreements; e.g. dictionaries, prior awards, judicial decisions, negotiating history and the practice of the parties

ambiguity doubtful or uncertain meaning; ordinarily used in connection with collective agreement language which is open to more than one interpretation; a patent ambiguity is one which is apparent on the face of the agreement, whereas a latent ambiguity is one that becomes apparent only after an examination of surrounding circumstances; extrinsic evidence is admissible to resolve an ambiguity; see **extrinsic evidence**

arbitrable capable of being arbitrated; the issue of **arbitrability**, i.e. whether a grievance falls within an arbitrator's jurisdiction or legal authority to decide, often arises where a party has failed to file the grievance within the time specified in the collective agreement

arbitral relating to arbitration; e.g. arbitral reasoning; **arbitral jurisprudence** is the body of collective agreement law contained in arbitration awards

arbitration adjudication of a dispute by an impartial third party, normally but not always, chosen by the parties themselves; labour arbitration involves the determination of disputes between labour and management by a sole arbitrator or board of arbitration; in Canada labour arbitration is conducted largely by arbitrators who are agreed to by the parties on an *ad hoc* basis, or who, failing agreement, are appointed by the government or a government agency, although in some jurisdictions, especially in the public sector, arbitration may be conducted to a limited extent by specialized tribunals

balance of probabilities measure of proof in civil proceedings, including arbitration and labour board cases, which requires a party to establish its case by the greater weight of evidence; the cogency of evidence that is required may vary, however, according to the nature of the allegation and the consequences of the proceeding

best evidence rule rule of evidence law which requires that the original of a document be presented in evidence unless it has been lost or destroyed or is otherwise unavailable; see **primary evidence**

bias prejudice, predisposition, partiality; bias in law occurs, not only where the arbitrator is biased in fact, but also where a party has a reasonable apprehension of bias

brief written summary; usually used to describe the written submissions of an advocate setting out the law and facts in support of a party's position; also used to describe the compendium of notes, memoranda, documents, etc. compiled by an advocate for his or her own use at a hearing

burden of proof obligation to prove one's case by affirmatively establishing the facts in dispute; the burden of proof in arbitration and other civil proceedings requires proof of the facts by a preponderance of evidence, whereas the burden of proof in criminal cases requires that the guilt of the accused be established beyond a reasonable doubt; **legal or persuasive burden of proof:** the burden of persuading the arbitrator that all elements of the case have been established, which never shifts from one party to the other during the proceedings, and which is generally upon the party making a claim or filing a grievance; however, where discipline or discharge is in issue at arbitration, the legal burden of proof is on the employer; **secondary or evidentiary burden of proof:** the burden of adducing evidence with respect to particular facts, which may shift from one party to the other during the course of the proceedings, depending upon such factors as the special knowledge which one party or the other may possess; see **standard of proof**

canons of construction general rules or maxims used to assist in the interpretation of statutes or written documents such as collective agreements; e.g. where a conflict exists between provisions in a collective agreement or statute, specific clauses override general clauses

circumstantial evidence indirect evidence; evidence of facts or circumstances which do not directly establish the existence of the facts in dispute, as would evidence based on personal knowledge or observation, but which render the facts in issue more probable, or from which the facts in issue may be inferred; contrast **direct evidence**

citation reference to sources of legal authority, including decisions of courts and arbitrators; the citation of decided cases in legal argument usually includes the name of the case, the year in which it was decided, the volume and page number of the report service, and the name of the court, tribunal or arbitrator making the decision, e.g. *Polymer Corp. Ltd.* (1958), 10 L.A.C. 31 (Laskin)

clear and cogent evidence measure of proof required where nature of allegation is serious and consequences are severe

climate of collective bargaining the context of labour relations practices and prior arbitration awards with which the parties are assumed to be familiar when they bargain a collective agreement; utilized by arbitrators as an aid to the interpretation of collective agreements; e.g. given that virtually all arbitrators permit employers to contract out bargaining unit work, collective agreements will be construed, in the light of this climate of collective bargaining, to permit contracting out in the absence of specific language to the contrary

collateral facts or issues   facts or issues which are not directly relevant to the facts or issues in dispute; ordinarily, in a legal dispute, evidence may not be presented with respect to collateral matters; although a witness may be cross-examined regarding collateral matters, the answers cannot be contradicted

compellability   liability to give evidence where required; one spouse cannot be compelled to testify against the other

compliance order   order made by an arbitrator requiring a party to comply with a collective agreement

conduct money   money paid to a witness subpoenaed to attend a hearing to defray the expenses of coming to, staying at and returning from the hearing; see subpoena and compare **witness fee**

continuing grievance   continuing or repeated breach of a collective agreement

corroboration   evidence strengthening testimony already given by confirming its accuracy; generally, corroborative evidence is not essential, but where it is required, as in the case of testimony by an accomplice, it must confirm in some material particular not only that an offence has been committed, but also that the accused person committed it

credibility   quality of a witness which renders the evidence worthy of belief; dependent upon a number of factors including the witness' demeanour, honesty and impartiality, reliability of memory, and capacity and opportunity to make exact and accurate observations; the most important factor is the consistency of the witness' testimony with the preponderance of probabilities in the light of surrounding circumstances

cross-examination   questioning of a witness called by the other party in a legal proceeding for the purpose of testing credibility and obtaining additional evidence; cross-examination, which may include questions of a leading nature, is not confined to matters addressed in examination-in-chief but may be directed to all matters that are relevant or go to credibility; compare **examination-in-chief** and **re-examination**

culminating incident   final act of misconduct by an employee without which discipline or discharge cannot normally be imposed under a collective agreement; under the culminating incident doctrine, once a final act of misconduct has been established, the employer may take into account the employee's previous disciplinary record in deciding upon the discipline to be imposed

demonstrative evidence evidence directed to the senses without the intervention of testimony; real evidence, i.e. things, such as photographs, diagrams, models, charts, x-rays, or physical objects, such as guns, clothing, etc.

direct evidence   evidence of a witness based on personal observation, rather than on inference or hearsay; contrast **circumstantial evidence**

directory   pertaining to a provision in a collective agreement which serves as a guideline only; non-compliance with a directory provision does not necessarily invalidate proceedings especially where there has been no prejudice to the opposite party; contrast **mandatory**

discovery   pre-hearing procedure by which one party can obtain relevant documents and information from the opposing party; while generally available in legal actions in the courts, there is no standard practice before arbitrators

documentary evidence   evidence in the form of documents such as correspondence, agreements, business records, etc.; public and judicial documents may be admissible without proof, but the authenticity, i.e. authorship or execution of other documents must be established before they are admissible and their contents can be relied upon

ejusdem generis   literally, of the same class; a rule of construction of documents and statutes to the effect that general words following specific words are to be restricted to the same class or category as the specific words; e.g. where a collective agreement provides that the employer shall furnish shoes, socks, uniforms and "all other employees' needs", the word "needs" is likely to be interpreted to refer to articles of clothing

error of law   legal error made by an arbitrator which may render a decision subject to judicial review where it appears on the face of the record, i.e. from a reading of the reasons for the decision and the pleadings or documents initiating the proceedings; errors of law include mistaken construction of a statute, incorrect application of rules of evidence or interpretation, patently unreasonable construction of a collective agreement, etc.; where a tribunal is protected by a statutory "privative clause" ousting the court's jurisdiction, a decision can be reviewed for error of law only where the error is jurisdictional in nature; see **jurisdictional error**

estoppel   principle of law preventing a party from insisting on its strict legal rights where by its words or conduct it has represented that it would not do so and another party has changed its position to its disadvantage or detriment in reliance upon that representation; for example, an employer, who has paid benefits without insisting on a waiting period stipulated in the collective agreement, may be estopped from subsequently altering such a practice before renegotiating the agreement; estoppel may be based not only on actual statements made by a party, but also on past practice, or a prior course of conduct, or even the failure of a party to grieve or object to a departure from the parties' strict legal rights or obligations; where estoppel involves rights under a collective agreement, the requirement of detrimental reliance may be satisfied if the party asserting the estoppel establishes that, in reliance on the other party's representations, it gave up the opportunity to negotiate a change in the collective agreement; although estoppel can be brought to an end by notice that a party intends to revert to its strict legal rights, arbitrators have generally held that the party adversely affected must first be given the opportunity to negotiate the issue in dispute;

evidence   proof of facts in legal proceedings which may consist of witnesses' testimony, documents, exhibits and other real evidence; the **law of evidence** comprises all the rules governing the presentation of facts and proof in legal proceedings including the rules governing the admissibility of evidence

examination-in-chief   questioning of a witness by the party which called the witness to give evidence, also referred to as direct examination; leading questions are ordinarily not permitted during examination-in-chief; compare **cross-examination** and **re-examination**

exclusionary rule   rule of the law of evidence excluding otherwise relevant evidence, e.g. rule against hearsay

exclusion of witnesses   order requiring potential witnesses to remain outside the hearing room until they are called to give evidence, in order that their testimony not be affected by the testimony of previous witnesses; see **adviser**

exhibit   document or physical object adduced as evidence in a legal proceeding or referred to in an affidavit

expert witness   witness possessing special skill or knowledge whose opinion is admissible in evidence on

matters falling within his or her expertise, such as a doctor or handwriting expert; see **opinion evidence**

expressio unius est exclusio alterius   literally, the express mention of one person or thing is the exclusion of another; when certain persons or things are specifically referred to in a statute or document, an intention may be inferred that all others are excluded from its operation; thus, where a collective agreement provides that hard hats are to be provided without charge by the employer, an inference may be drawn that employees will be required to pay for other safety equipment; courts and arbitrators have emphasized that the expressio unius maxim is "a valuable servant but a dangerous master" and must accordingly be applied with extreme caution

extrinsic evidence   evidence external to a collective agreement such as past practice or negotiating history; admissible to support an argument based on estoppel or to assist in the interpretation of a collective agreement where the language thereof is ambiguous; see **ambiguity** and **estoppel**

friend   form of address by which one lawyer refers to another in the course of legal proceedings

frustration   doctrine of contract law holding that parties may be relieved of their contractual obligations where unforeseeable circumstances occur which make it impossible, illegal or pointless to perform the contract

functus officio literally, having discharged one's duty; doctrine holding that, once a decision-maker has rendered a final decision on a matter, he or she is without authority to act further with respect thereto except to correct clerical errors; the doctrine does not prevent an arbitrator from completing the award by dealing with matters left unaddressed, or from expressly retaining jurisdiction for this purpose, nor does it preclude the arbitrator from subsequently explaining the decision, although it cannot be altered or amended; the doctrine is subject to express statutory provisions which extend a decision-maker's jurisdiction, or which empower the decision-maker to vary or reconsider a prior determination

grievance claim or complaint involving the interpretation, application or alleged violation of a collective agreement; **individual grievance**: grievance relating to an individual employee; **group grievance**: grievance relating to a group of employees similarly affected by the employer's action; **policy grievance**: grievance by a union which may involve a matter of general policy or of general application of the collective agreement; **union grievance**: sometimes used interchangeably with policy grievance, but also referring specifically to a grievance directly affecting the union, such as a failure to remit union dues

grievance procedure steps spelled out in a collective agreement for the handling of a grievance, usually starting with a written grievance at the shop-floor level, followed by meetings between union and management, after which the grievance may be referred to arbitration; time limits for the processing of a grievance are commonly provided for in collective agreements, but they may not be mandatory in all cases and, where labour relations legislation so provides, may in appropriate circumstances be extended by an arbitrator

headnote summary, prepared by the editors of a law report series, of the facts of the case, the issue involved, and the reasons for decision

hearsay evidence second-hand evidence; facts not in the personal knowledge of a witness, but rather information provided to the witness by another; as a general rule, such evidence is not admissible to prove the truth of facts, because the person who made the original statement is not in court and his or her credibility cannot therefore be tested by cross-examination; however, exceptions have been made to the rule against hearsay, such as admissions, business records, medical records, declarations as to physical or mental condition, testimony in former proceedings, etc.

hostile witness witness who discloses a hostile animus toward the party calling him or her and who may therefore be cross-examined; see adverse witness

hypothetical question question based on an assumption, or series of assumptions, that have not been proved; ordinarily permissible only in questioning expert witnesses

inadmissible evidence evidence which, according to legal rules, may not be admitted in a legal proceeding

inherent existing in and insepa-rable from; vested; inherent power is authority possessed without its being derived from another source; thus, the power of an arbitrator to award damages has been held to be inherent in the arbitration process, although it has also been implied s a term of the collective agreement

judicial notice recognition or acceptance by an arbitrator of indisputable facts without the necessity of formal proof; arbitrators take judicial notice of (1) matters of common knowledge in everyday life, such as the fact that union members will not ordinarily cross a picket line; (2) facts which are so notorious as not to be the subject of dispute among reasonable men and women, such as local conditions, geographi-cal facts, human behaviour and business and trade practices; (3) facts which are capable of immediate and accurate demonstration by resorting to readily accessible sources of indisputable accuracy, such as official matters, historical facts, time, measures and weights, the course of nature and scientific facts; in addition to the foregoing, specific statutes may provide that judicial notice can be taken of certain public records, legislative instruments and scientific or technical facts within a tribunal's specialized knowledge: see, for example, the Evidence Acts, the Interpretation Acts, and the Ontario Statutory Powers Procedure Act

judicial review review by a superior court of a decision of an arbitrator or statutory tribunal to ensure that these bodies properly exercise the jurisdiction or authority conferred upon them by legislation; judicial review is not an appeal, so that the courts will not intervene except where there has been (1) a denial of a fair hearing (2) a jurisdic-tional error or (3) in the absence of a privative clause ousting the court's jurisdiction, an error of law on the face of the record; the ground for interven-tion most frequently cited   by the courts in quashing arbitration awards is a patently unreasonable construc-tion of a collective agreement by the arbitrator; see **error of law**, **jurisdic-tional error**, **natural justice**

jurisdiction legal power and authority of an arbitrator to hear and determine a case; jurisdiction may be over subject matter, parties or location, and it may be **exclusive** or **concurrent**, i.e. exercised solely by one body or shared with other bodies

jurisdictional error legal error committed by a body which declines to exercise its authority, or exceeds or abuses the power conferred upon it by statute; a ground for intervention by the court; see **judicial review**

leading case decision or prece-dent commonly accepted as clarify-ing or settling the principles relating to a particular legal issue; a leading case may be of such importance as to constitute a **landmark case**, it may be referred to as a **bellwether** case if it is consistently followed, or it may signal such a departure from established principles as to amount to a **watershed** case

leading question question which suggests an answer to the witness or assumes the existence of disputed facts to which the witness is to testify; generally a party is not allowed to ask leading questions of its own witness, unless the witness has been declared hostile, or the questions relate to matters not in dispute; however, leading questions are permissible in cross-examination

mandatory obligatory, imperative; a mandatory provision in a statute or collective agreement is one which, if not followed, renders the proceedings to which it relates void; mandatory time limits in the grievance and arbitration provisions of a collective agreement are time limits which, if not complied with, will result in dismissal of the grievance; however, the time limits may be waived by the other party, and the delay may be excused by an arbitrator pursuant to legislation which, in some jurisdictions, allows an arbitrator to extend time limits or cure irregularities; contrast **directory**

merits the substance of a party's claim or defence; the real matter in dispute

minutes of settlement document signed by the parties recording terms of settlement of a matter that is the subject of a legal claim or action

natural justice procedural fairness; requirement applicable to tribunal such as arbitration board when making decisions that affect the rights and interests of individuals; the rules of natural justice require that persons affected by a decision be notified of the case against them and be given a reasonable opportunity of presenting their case, and that the body making the decision listen fairly to both sides and reach a decision untainted by bias; the precise content of natural justice varies according to the nature of the power exercised, the decision involved, and the consequences that flow therefrom

negotiating history history of collective bargaining between parties to a collective agreement; includes previous collective agreements, negotiating proposals, statements made during bargaining; admissible at arbitration for the purpose of resolving an ambiguity in a collective agreement or of supporting an argument based upon estoppel; see **estoppel** and extrinsic evidence

obiter dictum literally, a saying by the way; a passing or incidental statement; an opinion contained in a decision that is not essential for disposition of the case, and which therefore is not binding as precedent; contrast *ratio decidendi*

objection to evidence opposition to the admissibility of evidence on the ground that it is irrelevant, or violates the rule against hearsay, or one of the other rules of evidence

opening statement address ordinarily delivered by an advocate at the outset of the case containing a summary of the alleged facts and the legal position of the party represented

opinion evidence   evidence of a witness' views or conclusions, as distinguished from his or her personal knowledge of the facts; ordinarily admissible in legal proceedings only if given by an expert witness, i.e. a person qualified as an expert by the possession of special skills and knowledge, derived from education or experience or both, which the ordinary person cannot be expected to possess; non-expert witnesses may, however, testify to such matters as age, speed of vehicles, handwriting or identity; see **expert witness**

particulars   material facts upon which a party bases its case; in proper circumstances, a party may be required by an arbitrator to provide particulars of its case to the opposite party, but it will not generally be required to disclose the evidence by which the particulars are to be proved

past practice   conduct or behaviour of the parties under a collective agreement with respect to a matter in dispute; evidence relating to past practice is admissible at arbitration to resolve an ambiguity in the collective agreement, or to show that one of the parties represented that it would not insist upon the strict terms of the agreement; see **estoppel** and **extrinsic evidence**

peremptory   final, conclusive, not open to challenge; a peremptory hearing date is the date set by the arbitrator on which the hearing will definitely proceed without further postponement

perfunctory   superficial, mechanical; perfunctory treatment of a grievance by a union may amount to a failure by the union to fulfill its duty of fair representation

pleadings   written statements exchanged by the parties during the course of litigation which set out the gist of each party's case including the material facts and the remedy requested; pleadings in an arbitration case include the grievance and reply thereto

precedent   decision of a court or tribunal that is considered as authority for deciding similar cases subsequently in accordance with the same principles; under the **doctrine of precedent** cases decided by a higher court which lay down a rule of law are authoritative and must be followed when the same point arises again in litigation; however, neither arbitrators nor labour boards are bound to follow prior arbitration awards on the same issue, although labour boards generally show a keen regard for consistency because of their institutional structure; see *obiter dictum, ratio decidendi, res judicata*

preliminary objection   objection, ordinarily made at the outset of a hearing, relating to the jurisdiction of an arbitrator to entertain a grievance

preponderance of evidence   standard of proof used in civil cases and arbitration proceedings which requires that the party having the burden of proof establish the facts in issue by the greater weight of the evidence; see **balance of probabilities**

presumption inference or assumption; a **presumption of fact** is an inference of fact from known facts, whereas a **presumption of law** is a supposition that the law allows or requires to be made, e.g. that a person accused of a crime is innocent until proved guilty, or that a child of tender years is incapable of committing a crime; a presumption may be conclusive or irrebuttable, in the sense that it cannot be overcome by any evidence, argument or consideration, or it may be rebuttable, in the sense that it holds good only in the absence of contrary evidence

prima facie literally, at first sight, on the face of things; a *prima facie* **case** is a case that has been supported in essential respects by sufficient evidence for it to be taken as proved in the absence of adequate evidence to the contrary; prima facie evidence is (1) evidence which tends to prove a fact, but does not do so conclusively; (2) evidence which is of sufficient weight to require the opposite party to answer it and which, unless explained or contradicted, may be sufficient to establish the facts in issue; see **burden of proof**

primary evidence original or best evidence; the rule that a party must adduce the best evidence that the nature of the case will allow is now confined to proof of documents in the sense that a party is required to adduce the original of a document as evidence unless the original has been lost or destroyed or is in the possession of another party who refuses to produce it or from whom it cannot reasonably be obtained; see **best evidence rule**

prior inconsistent statement prior contradictory statement by a witness which is ordinarily used to impeach the witness' credibility

privilege (1) exceptional or extraordinary advantage; immunity or exemption; (2) rule of evidence law protecting confidential communications from disclosure in a legal proceeding without consent, e.g. communications between a solicitor and client, or settlement discussions during the grievance procedure

probative tending to prove or actually proving facts; the **probative value** of evidence is the extent to which it tends to prove an issue in dispute; **probative evidence** is generally admissible save in those limited circumstances where its probative value is out-weighed by its prejudicial effect

procedural fairness due process; requirement that an individual who may be affected by a decision of a tribunal is entitled to procedural protections, including, as a minimum, notice of the essential elements of the opposite party's case, and an opportunity to present one's case before an unbiased body; see **natural justice**

procedural objection objection relating to a matter of procedure, rather than a matter of substantive law; **see substantive law**

procedure mode of proceeding by which a legal right is enforced; includes the law of evidence, the rules prescribing formal steps in a legal proceeding, the remedies available

production   procedure whereby a party is required upon request to produce for inspection to the other party all documents in its possession, custody or power which may be relevant to the issues in dispute

quantum   literally, how much; amount; where liability is established, arbitrators usually retain jurisdiction to deal with the quantum of compensation in the event the parties are unable to agree; the quantum of compensation will ordinarily be fixed in an amount sufficient to place the aggrieved party in a monetary position as near as possible to that in which he or she would have been had the wrong not occurred

ratio decidendi   literally, reason for deciding; those principles which constitute the basis of a decision; contrast **obiter dictum**

real evidence   evidence, other than testimony or documents, produced at a hearing, including material objects, such as a piece of machinery; see **demonstrative evidence**

rebut   refute, disprove; **rebuttal evidence** is evidence introduced by one party in a legal proceeding to explain, contradict or disprove evidence given by the other party

rectification   legal remedy where the courts may correct an error in a contract where the parties shared a common agreement regarding the terms of the contract, but recorded them incorrectly; controversy exists as to whether arbitrators or labour boards possess the authority to grant this remedy

re-examination   questioning by an advocate of a witness called by that advocate, after the cross-examination, upon matters arising out of the cross-examination; compare **examination-in-chief** and **cross-examination**

refreshing memory   enhancement of a witness' recollection of past events by referring to documents which came into being at or near the time of the occurrence of the event or matter recorded

relevant   pertinent, germane, applying to the matter in question; evidence must be relevant to be admissible in a legal proceeding, i.e. it must tend to prove or disprove a fact in issue, but not all relevant evidence is admissible; see **exclusionary rule**

remedy   means by which a right is enforced or the violation of a right is prevented or compensated; such means may include, for example, reinstatement, compensation, direction, declaration, etc.

reply   statement by a party in answer to the opposite party's case; **reply evidence** is rebuttal evidence presented by a party following the opposite party's case in order to contradict or qualify facts raised for the first time; **reply argument** is rebuttal argument made by a party following the opposite party's argument in order to explain or refute new matters; the **right of reply** is the right of an advocate in a case to have the last word or to make the last address before a decision is rendered

res gestae   literally, the things done; facts surrounding an incident which is the subject of a legal proceeding; statements or declarations which accompany and explain an act or event in issue, which may be admissible as evidence, even though hearsay in nature

res judicata literally, matter or thing decided; legal defence that a final decision between the same parties regarding the cause of action is conclusive as between them so that it cannot be relitigated by the original parties except on the ground of fraud; the doctrine, which is based on the need for finality of litigation, is applicable to court actions, but not to proceedings before arbitrators or other administrative tribunals, such as labour boards, although such bodies seldom depart from a previous decision between the same parties on the same issue

retain jurisdiction maintain power or authority to deal with a matter in dispute; arbitrators frequently retain jurisdiction, if liability is established, to determine issues which may arise with respect to quantum of compensation, among other matters

rules of evidence legal rules governing the admissibility of evidence in legal proceedings; see **admissible evidence**

self-incrimination acts or declarations by which a person implicates himself or herself in an offence; a witness cannot under Canadian law refuse to answer a question on the ground that the answer might tend to incriminate him or her; the witness' testimony cannot be used to incriminate him or her in any subsequent proceeding except prosecution for perjury, but it may be used to discredit his or her evidence

self-serving term used to describe statements made by a person following an event in dispute and prior to the hearing which serve to confirm the person's version of the event; ordinarily such statements are considered inadmissible

similar fact evidence evidence of similar misconduct by a party on other occasions in the past; admissible only if a special connection exists relating the facts in issue to the evidence tendered and its value as evidence does not outweigh its prejudicial effect

standard of proof degree of proof necessary to establish a fact; in arbitration and other civil proceedings facts must be established by a preponderance of evidence, i.e. on a balance of probabilities; the degree of proof required varies depending upon the nature of the offence and the seriousness of the consequences, e.g. where conduct of a criminal nature is alleged in the context of arbitration, clear and cogent evidence is required; see **burden of proof**

subpoena literally, under penalty; summons issued under authority of an arbitrator requiring the person to whom it is directed to attend a hearing at a specified time and place for the purpose of giving evidence, subject to a penalty for non-attendance; a **subpoena ad testificandum** requires the witness to attend and give oral testimony, whereas a **subpoena duces tecum** requires the witness not only to attend and give evi-

202 WINNING CASES AT GRIEVANCE ARBITRATION

dence, but also to bring with him or her documents under the witness' control which are specified in the subpoena; see **conduct money** and **witness fee**

substantive law creates rights and duties, whereas **adjectival** or **procedural** law prescribes the legal machinery by which the substantive law is determined or enforced

summons command to appear before an arbitrator at a specified time and place

testimony oral evidence given by a witness under oath

time limit period of time specified by collective agreement or statute within which an act must be performed; collective agreements commonly contain time limits for the filing and processing of grievances and for their referral to arbitration; whether a breach of such time limits will result in dismissal of the grievance depends upon whether they are directory or mandatory, have been waived by the other party, or are extended by an arbitrator pursuant to a power conferred by collective agreement or statute

view, taking a inspection by an arbitrator, with the parties present, of an object, property or place outside the hearing with respect to which a question arises in the course of the proceeding

viva voce literally, with living voice; oral; used ordinarily to describe oral evidence given by a witness under oath

waiver voluntary or intentional relinquishment or surrender of a

right, claim, privilege or advantage; waiver may arise from words or conduct, and implies an intention to forego or abandon a condition which has not been complied with by the other party; thus, for example, where an employer participates in processing a grievance to arbitration, without objecting to a breach of time limits, a waiver may be inferred; see **estoppel**

weight of evidence value of evidence; preponderance of evidence

withdraw remove, take back, discontinue; to withdraw a grievance is to discontinue it without the consent or agreement of the other party

without prejudice expression used to indicate that a person or party making an offer or taking an action does so on the basis that the offer or action does not imply an admission of liability, or otherwise adversely affect his or her legal rights; settlement discussions between a union and an employer during the grievance procedure are inadmissible in evidence, whether or not such discussions are stated to be without prejudice, because as a matter of policy it is in the interest of sound labour relations to encourage a frank exchange of information

witness (1) one who testifies to what he or she has seen, heard or otherwise observed; (2) one who, being present, personally sees or perceives a thing

witness fee money paid to a witness subpoenaed to attend a hearing as compensation for loss of time; see **subpoena** and compare **conduct money**

Index